The Debt-Free Church is a challenging book that addresses a challenging issue facing many churches. The authors have done their homework, and I especially appreciate the spirit with which they communicate their message. I heartily recommend *The Debt-Free Church* to anyone seeking the Lord's direction in ministry expansion.

Howard Dayton
Founder, Crown Ministries
Longwood, Florida

THE
DEBT-FREE
CHURCH

EXPERIENCING
FINANCIAL FREEDOM
WHILE GROWING
YOUR MINISTRY

JEFF BERG & JIM BURGESS
FOREWORD BY LARRY BURKETT

MOODY PRESS
CHICAGO

ISBN: 0-8024-2286-1

5 7 9 10 8 6 4

Printed in the United States of America

CONTENTS

To the glory of God,
we dedicate this book to
our friend and mentor
Larry Burkett,
who has helped us and our families
in ways that only eternity will reveal;

and with **very special thanks** to our wives
Janet Berg and Alanda Burgess,
who supported us with encouragement, help,
suggestions, counsel, and patience
far beyond any reasonable expectation;

with additional thanks to:

Tom Wells,
for research, support, encouragement, and priceless input;

Bob Frank,
for input, prayer, and tireless encouragement;

the elders of Circle Community Church
and Fellowship Bible Church,
for their support, encouragement, input, and patience;

and to Greg Thornton
and the patient, skillful, and dedicated staff of Moody Press
for giving us this opportunity.

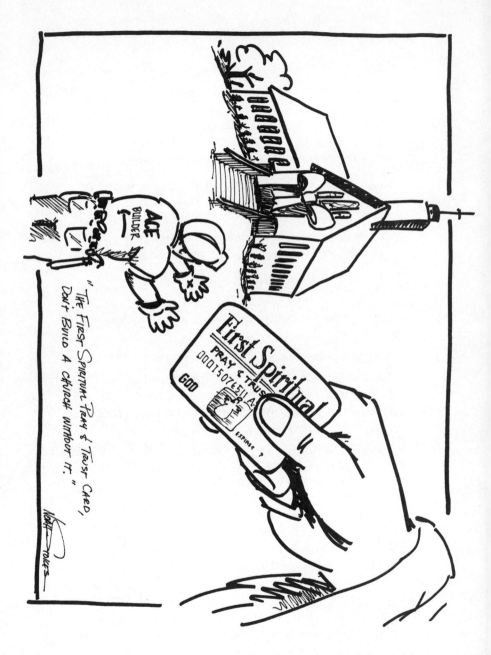

FOREWORD

Fifty-nine percent of America's churches plan to either build an addition or embark on a major renovation in the near future, making fund-raising a crucial ministry issue. Decisions to borrow likely will entangle churches with loan repayments for years to come, while other ministry opportunities are missed due to lack of funds. There is an alternative. Jeff Berg and Jim Burgess have written *The Debt-Free Church* to challenge our nation's churches to trust God to supply the finances needed for ministry. This practical resource provides a complete overview of the biblical principles of debt, case studies of churches that have built debt-free, as well as strategies to help churches accelerate their loan repayments. In addition, one chapter provides solid, biblical answers to the most common reasons churches are tempted to borrow in the first place.

Those who have followed the ministry of Christian Financial Concepts know how deeply I desire God's people to be a faithful witness to His glory and power. Operating debt-free as a church requires great courage and faith in God's sufficiency, but it provides a powerful testimony to our materialistic culture. Jeff and Jim not only will inspire you to lead your church to her greatest potential, but they will also demonstrate how it can be done practically.

As the federal government continues to whittle away human services due to lack of funds, opportunities will increase for God's church to serve basic human needs. Churches that are debt-free will be the most flexible and should be prepared to respond to these rapidly changing conditions. Will your church be ready—free from all entangling obligations?

The Debt-Free Church is strategic reading for every pastor, church leader, finance committee, and church member. As we approach the close of this century, I believe God will use this book as an effective tool to prepare His church to be a faithful witness.

LARRY BURKETT
Founder and President
Christian Financial Concepts

WHY THIS BOOK?
Exploring the Challenge of Debt-Free Ministry

We have written this book for the purpose of challenging, encouraging, and exhorting Christians (both corporately and individually) to operate debt-free. Our motive is to glorify God through helping enable the body of Christ to experience financial freedom; and as a result, to minister more effectively. Our three-fold mission is to:

1. *Challenge* churches and ministries to be debt-free by relating the actual experiences of pastors and ministry leaders whose healthy, growing ministries are debt-free—or are becoming debt-free.

2. *Encourage* churches and ministries to be debt-free by accurately and compassionately communicating the principles and models of debt-free ministry that are presented in the Bible.

3. *Exhort* individual Christians to be debt-free so they can be more effective in their personal ministries, their family ministries, and in supporting their local churches.

In Matthew 6:21 and Luke 16:10–12, Christ explains that people demonstrate what they really believe by how

they spend their money. As Larry Burkett, founder of
Christian Financial Concepts, often says, "How we use our
money is an outward indicator of our spiritual condition."

So what does it really mean when Christians borrow
money to fund ministry efforts? What does it say about the
spiritual condition of America's congregations when 90
percent of our church buildings are constructed by means
of borrowed funds? This book is an attempt to answer
questions such as these in a biblical and practical way.

This book is also our attempt to awaken Christians to
the importance of living and ministering debt-free. We believe we can demonstrate from Scripture, as well as from
current practical experience, that being debt-free is not an
"impossible dream." Rather, it is God's *best and highest
way of doing things,* and, we believe, one of His great desires for His people.

What this book is not. We realize that when we raise the
issue of debt-free ministry, we'll raise controversy. That's
why we think it's also important to stress what this book
does *not* do:

1. This book does *not* teach that borrowing money is
   sinful. Nowhere in the Bible does God indicate that
   borrowing is sinful. We believe that borrowing (especially for ministry purposes) is always risky, often wasteful, and almost always unwise—but it's
   not a sin.

2. This book does *not* seek to condemn or discourage
   anyone involved with a ministry that is currently
   in debt. Nor do we condemn or discourage families, individuals, or ministries that are repaying
   borrowed money. We believe that all Christians
   will be happier and enjoy greater blessing from
   God if they can become debt-free. Yet we know
   that many don't share our conviction. And while
   we may disagree with them, we certainly don't
   want to condemn them.

3. This book does *not* encourage you to automatically
   forsake your church or ministry if it borrows mon-

ey. In most cases, we recommend that you stay. After all, how will a ministry ever become financially free if there is no one to pray, to model, and to encourage debt-free ministry?

4. This book does *not* seek to discourage wise, careful, God-directed building programs or ministry expansions. We believe that ministry growth is often a sign of God's blessing, but we believe borrowed funds are *not* a requirement for growing ministries.

5. This book does *not* seek to divide Christians over the issue of ministering debt-free. There are already far too many divisions in the body of Christ. The last problem we need is a wall of division between the borrowers and non-borrowers. *Please* do not use the information in this book to create divisions or factions within the family of God (Colossians 3:14–15).

Not a new problem. Borrowing for ministry purposes is not a new problem; Christians have been wrestling with the issue for generations. J. Hudson Taylor was one of history's great Christians and a landmark missionary pioneer. As the founder of the China Inland Mission (now Overseas Missionary Fellowship), Taylor opened the most heavily populated nation on earth to the gospel. Even today, Taylor is widely respected for his faith and insight. It was his firm conviction that God's work, done in God's way, would never lack for God's provision.

Taylor shared his conviction that the China Inland Mission should never borrow money:

> It is really just as easy for God to give beforehand; and He prefers to do so. He is too wise to allow His purpose to be frustrated for lack of a little money; but money wrongly placed or obtained in unspiritual ways is sure to hinder blessing.
>
> And what does going into debt really mean? It means that God has not supplied your need. You trusted Him, but He has not given you the money; so you supply yourself, and borrow. If we can only wait right up to the time, God cannot lie, God cannot forget: He is pledged to supply all your need.[1]

We pray that Christians—especially those who may have never carefully thought through the issue of debt-free ministry—will read this book with an open mind. We hope you'll agree with us that debt-free ministry is God's will for all believers. So be encouraged. It's not an impossible dream—you too can be a part of a vibrant, growing, debt-free ministry!

Meet the authors. We're Jeff Berg and Jim Burgess. As volunteer financial counselors and seminar instructors for Christian Financial Concepts, we've been responding to questions about ministry borrowing for years. In addition, Jeff serves as an elder at Circle Community Church in Orlando, Florida, and Jim is the lead pastor and an elder at Fellowship Bible Church in Dalton, Georgia. As this manuscript was being completed, we were both in the process of helping lead our churches through debt-free ministry expansions. So for those of you who are striving to help your ministries be debt-free, take comfort. We know what you're going through.

Both of us contributed equally to this book, and we've written in the first person plural. So when you read "we've seen" or "we believe," we're referring to what either or both of us believe or have experienced. Occasionally, when we're writing specifically about our individual experiences, we refer to simply "Jeff" or "Jim" and use the third person "he."

The opinions expressed in this book are our own. In fact, the more we worked together, the more delighted we became at how closely we agree on the issue of ministry borrowing and its impact on the church. We began this project as acquaintances; we finish as close friends.

We appreciate the time you're taking to read this book. Although you may not agree with every point we make, we hope and pray that you come away blessed and challenged.

NOTE

1. Dr. and Mrs. Howard Taylor, *Hudson Taylor and China Inland Mission: The Growth of a Work of God,* vol. 2 (Singapore: Overseas Missionary Fellowship, 1918; reprinted 1988), 54.

CHAPTER 1

THE CHURCH SET FREE
Experiencing the Joy of Debt-Free Ministry

Churches and ministries all across America are experiencing the joy of being debt-free. Those that perform God's work without borrowing money are experiencing the peace that comes from following biblical principles. Debt-free ministries are seeing God work in powerful ways for which only He can get the glory. And debt-free ministries are realizing impressive spiritual, financial, and ministry benefits.

Debt-free ministries can be found throughout America, ranging in size from fewer than 100 to nearly 10,000 members, and coming from many denominations.

PROFILES IN DEBT-FREE MINISTRY

According to the dozens of pastors and ministry leaders we have interviewed, trusting God to provide a ministry's needs *without borrowing money* is an exciting, challenging, and rewarding adventure of faith.

Virtually every debt-free ministry we have spoken to in the last several years has been delighted to be debt-free. Pastors, elders, deacons, administrators, and folks in the pews get excited when they are involved in a healthy, well-balanced ministry that is debt-free. The pastor of one of

America's largest debt-free churches told us, "Our people are so thrilled with what we see happening as a result of being out of debt [that] we will never go back to borrowing."

We discovered infectious enthusiasm and creativity in debt-free ministries. As a result, it was difficult for us to decide which ones to profile here. The debt-free ministries we talked to were all eager for us to tell the stories of what God has done for them.

There are many uplifting ministry tales to tell, and we've tried to weave as many as possible into the fabric of this book. But after much discussion and prayer, we decided to open this chapter with profiles of only four debt-free ministries:

- Denton Bible Church (Denton, Texas)
- Harvest Christian Fellowship (Spokane, Washington)
- Grace Bible Fellowship (Walpole, New Hampshire)
- RBC Ministries (Grand Rapids, Michigan)

Profile 1—Denton Bible Church

Denton Bible Church is a vital, thriving ministry located some thirty-five miles north of Dallas in the town of Denton. With an attendance of more than 2,500 adults, the church is making an impact in the lives of people around the world. The twenty-three-acre campus includes a large educational facility and a new $1.5 million chapel. All church land and buildings have been funded by cash from congregational giving, with the exception of the ministry's first facility.

But debt-free ministry did not come to Denton without sacrifice. Nor could it have even been achieved without the determined leadership of founding pastor Mel Sumrall, whose commitment to debt-free growth did not go untested—especially in the church's early years.

From Manager to Minister. Sumrall had been the manager of a large Colorado steel plant and was only five years from retirement when God called him into the ministry. Denton Bible Church grew out of a Bible study that Sumrall started in 1976 while a student at Dallas Theological

Seminary. One of his assignments as a ministerial student was to work in Denton with a group of twelve people who were interested in forming a church. With very little experience and no major church or denominational backing, Sumrall began to lead the fledgling work.

Initially they met in rented facilities, but in 1978 the 100-member congregation had an opportunity to purchase land for $42,500. They decided to make a $22,000 down payment and raise the remainder of the money within one year. At the time the task seemed enormous, but Sumrall was confident that God would meet their need.

The congregation, composed largely of college students from a local university, didn't have much money. But the people were willing to give sacrificially. Some students sold musical instruments, stereos, and other personal belongings and donated the proceeds. Others in the church also caught the vision and gave repeatedly and generously. Before the year was up, the rest of the money had been raised.

Heave-Ho for Cold Cash. What fund-raising methods does the church use now? Not traditional ones. For example, Denton Bible has never taken an offering by "passing the plate." Instead, church leaders trust that God's Spirit will move people to deposit their gifts in the offering boxes located at the back of the church. The people have responded with generous and sacrificial giving to meet every need. And when special offerings are taken (such as for phased, pay-as-you-go building programs) an ice chest is placed on a table and the people are asked to "Heave-Ho for Cold Cash." On one particular Sunday in December 1994, the church collected more than $100,000 in this way.

To build its first building in 1979, Denton Bible raised $20,000 in cash. When the church was offered a loan at the Federal Reserve discount rate, it reluctantly borrowed $80,000 from a bank—but with a commitment to repay the loan as soon as possible. For a time the new building even went without heat and furnishings, but the loan was paid back in 1982—less than three years later.

Since then, Denton Bible has never borrowed another penny. Yet the congregation's cash-in-hand purchases include the previously mentioned educational building and chapel, as well as two temporary buildings, a house, and twenty-three acres of land.

Debt-Free Ministry Benefits. Denton Bible's non-borrowing philosophy has brought the church significant benefits. According to Pastor Sumrall, the church enjoys "tremendous freedom to minister as God leads, and the opportunity to have ministries that would otherwise be impossible."[1] For example, Denton Bible supports twenty-one full-time pastors and an active youth ministry (with plans for a $300,000 debt-free youth ranch), as well as outreaches to the poor, the black and Hispanic communities, university students, and more.

Recently the church began a new ministry called "Church on the Square," which meets in an old converted theater on the town's historic square. This contemporary-themed, Saturday-night worship service is having notable impact. Denton Bible also has a missions program that supports a dozen Bible training centers in various countries around the world. "All of these ministries have been made possible because of our debt-free commitment," affirms Sumrall. "We simply could not be doing these things if we were in debt."

Tom Nelson, the church's current senior pastor, summarized the view of Denton Bible leadership about borrowing money to do God's work. "If you get a loan, your congregation never has to trust God, they just trust the bank," he said. "And when it's all over, they look around and say, 'Look at what the bank built.' When they say, 'Praise God for what He did,' there's an asterisk beside it. But when you build debt-free and say, 'Praise God,' there's no asterisk. It's *all* God's doing."[2]

Profile 2—Harvest Christian Fellowship

An 800-member downtown church, Harvest Christian Fellowship is a non-denominational, independent, charismatic congregation and one of the larger churches in Spokane, Washington. At the same location since 1973, the church now owns almost an entire city block. Over the years the church has built and remodeled several times, usually with borrowed funds. But all that changed in February 1993.

According to John Sonneland, Harvest's pastor of music and finance, the church was started in 1971 by young people who emerged from the West-Coast Jesus movement. The congregation gradually grew to more than two hundred, and in 1984, current senior pastor Steve Allen came on board.

Under Pastor Allen's leadership, the congregation began positioning itself to serve its community and other area churches as God led. The church developed a vision for the lost around the world and became the sending agency for missionaries to several foreign lands. In 1989 Harvest developed an innovative, one-year young-adult discipleship program called the Master's Commission, which now draws participants from as far away as Slovakia and Finland. In addition, church leadership began to feel more and more uncomfortable about repaying loans with interest.

The "Tithing Revival." In February 1993, something exciting began to happen. The pastoral staff was feeling burdened about the facilities "squeeze" and was looking for ways to expand.

Sparked by one of its five full-time pastors, the entire pastoral team became concerned about the state of giving in their own lives as well as in the church at large. Together they began an in-depth study of biblical financial principles. As a result of their study, the pastors also became burdened about their lack of financial teaching from the pulpit. "We repented of that," remembered Sonneland. "It wasn't right. Jesus talked about our money; Jesus talked about our stewardship. And if we can't be faithful in the little things—like money—how can God trust us with spiritual things?"

One Sunday, all of the pastors confessed their poor giving leadership in front of the entire congregation during a special, emotion-filled morning service. The pastors pledged that they were each recommitting their personal finances to the church's ministry. In addition, new ministry programs just starting up were put "on hold" until God began to work in the hearts of His people to give. At that time, an estimated 40 percent of the Harvest congregation was regularly tithing (giving 10 percent of their income).

The result of this open, dramatic confession and scriptural challenge was truly spectacular: Offerings *more than doubled* the very next Sunday! And they kept increasing, until by April 1995 *more than 90 percent* of the congregation was tithing consistently.

With offerings more than doubled, the church was faced with a joyous dilemma: deciding how to use God's surplus. The pastors saw the loans and their accompanying interest payments as a barrier to complete effectiveness for the Lord. "All of us viewed the loans as a hindrance to ministry," recalled Sonneland. "We had always wanted to pay them off. Our philosophy is to sow our money into people, not things." The church decided to pay off the loans, redirect the principal and interest payments back into ministry, expand its discipleship program, and start new foreign mission projects.

Harvest initiated an aggressive loan repayment strategy, with full congregational support. As each loan was paid off, that payment was applied to the next loan. By June 1994, the church was totally debt-free!

As Harvest moves toward the twenty-first century, the church plans to build further on its ministry distinctives: a strong pro-life focus, young-adult discipleship, foreign missions, financial counseling, outreach to single mothers, and even community drama teams. And a congregation made up almost completely of tithers will enable the church to expand its ministry without the burdens and constraints that often accompany borrowing. According to Sonneland, only a financially free church is ideally positioned to minister to hurting people. "Being debt-free is God's biblical plan—and it works," he affirmed.

"It may take time," he said, "but if pastors fulfill their calling to hold people accountable to biblical standards of tithing and giving, God will fund whatever He wants to do in a ministry. The funding is already there; it's within the people—not only in their finances, but in their gifts, abilities, and talents. It's a matter of ministry leaders unlocking that treasure and helping people fulfill their own purposes and ministries. It's calling people to maturity in Christ."

Sonneland also has a word for America's church leaders: "We pastors have failed—we underchallenge people. We've been weak. We haven't called our people to a higher standard. We've given up and said 'It's easier to go to the bank and get money' or 'It's easier not to make people uncomfortable by calling them to tithe and give.' Pastors need to *challenge their people*. The resources are there, but pastors need the courage to call them forth from their people."

Profile 3—Grace Bible Fellowship

Located near the Connecticut River, which forms the boundary between New Hampshire and Vermont, tiny Grace Bible Fellowship has been debt-free since its inception in 1983. Not wanting to invest money in land or buildings, the twenty-family church rents the local town hall as its meeting place.

According to Pastor John Thompson, the cost is more than reasonable. "In the early days, we paid $10 per month, including utilities," he said. "Recently, they raised the rent to $15."

About half of the congregation drives over the river from Vermont, and Thompson says there is a friendly rivalry between the two states. Folks from New Hampshire jokingly say that the best thing about living in Vermont is being able to see their state on the other side of the river. Church members are more serious, however, when it comes to the subject of borrowing money.

The Philosophy of Debt-Free Ministry. All the members agree that their "borrow-free" policy is based on the wisdom of Scripture. "We have pursued a debt-free practice on the basis of philosophy, not pragmatism," Thompson stated. "From the Scripture we have seen that this is the right way to live according to God's principles. And by practicing this approach, we have seen God's overwhelming provision and enablement."

Thompson observed that the early church grew dramatically without the buildings that seem so necessary to today's congregations. "Besides," he said, "the Lord's house is not a building—it's His people."

Investing in People. It's in *people* that Thompson and the leadership of Grace Bible have chosen to invest their resources. Many small churches struggle to pay both pastor and mortgage. Because Grace Bible pays no mortgage, Thompson can earn a full-time salary that allows him to devote his full time to ministry.

As is common with healthy, well-balanced, debt-free churches, innovative ministry is also a Grace Bible distinctive. For example, the church recently had two women on staff whose mission was to go house to house, discipling the young mothers in the congregation. "We believe this [type of ministry] will pay tremendous spiritual dividends in the future," Thompson predicts. And largely because it is debt-free, the church can sponsor other important ministries, including a no-charge community counseling ministry, a community food bank, a strong discipleship program, and a significant investment in foreign missions.

The town hall building is getting a little cramped, and at some point in the future, God may open the door for a building program. But for now, the members of Grace Bible Fellowship believe that the cost of their own building would place an unwelcome drain on funds earmarked for a more important need: *ministry.*[3]

Profile 4—RBC Ministries

Although this book is oriented toward church leaders and congregations, churches are not the only kind of debt-free Christian ministry. Many parachurch ministries are also committed to operating without borrowing money.

One such parachurch organization is RBC Ministries (formerly Radio Bible Class—founded 1938) of Grand Rapids, Michigan. Many are familiar with its monthly devotional booklet *Our Daily Bread,* which is distributed free by thousands of churches throughout the world. Others know RBC from its uplifting and encouraging *Day of Discovery* television broadcast. For nearly sixty years, RBC has ministered with excellence and compassion to millions through radio, print, and television—all without borrowing money.

Dennis J. DeHaan, contributing editor of *Our Daily Bread,* said that the ministry's founder (his uncle), Dr. M. R. DeHaan, took a dim view of borrowing money to do God's work. According to the younger DeHaan, his uncle used to say that if enough support didn't come in, that was the Lord's signal to either cut back or "close up shop." And that is how RBC has always operated. Even when charitable donations dropped off dramatically after the infamous televangelist scandals of the late 1980s, RBC did not experience that same level of giving decline. The ministry has earned the long-term financial trust of its supporters by refusing loans, avoiding excesses, carefully managing its resources, and trusting God to provide.

RBC is just one of many examples of the kind of non-borrowing ministry that is becoming more and more prevalent across America. And it's happening because Christians are becoming increasingly concerned about fully trusting God to supply their ministry needs, then investing in the lives of people—rather than throwing money away in interest payments.

UNDERSTANDING THE TERMINOLOGY

As we move forward in our discussion of debt-free ministry, it's important that we pause to lay some groundwork. We first need to establish a solid understanding of the terminology we will use throughout this book. Understanding much of what follows depends upon having a clear definition of certain key terms:

- Financial freedom
- Borrow
- Lend
- Debt
- Surety
- Usury

Some define these terms in different ways. Opinions may vary, but for the sake of consistency, here are our

working definitions for key terms that appear throughout
The Debt-Free Church:

Financial Freedom

Financial freedom is when one is free from being enslaved to financial concerns. Financial enslavement can
take several forms: physical, emotional, mental, or spiritual.
In most cases, the loss of financial freedom is self-inflicted
through the nonapplication or misapplication of godly financial principles.

Financial freedom is an achievable goal, which you can
reach regardless of your current financial condition. We
define financial freedom as *living by wise financial principles and entrusting your total financial situation to God.*
When you are financially free, you experience inner contentment with no financial burdens (e.g., loans to repay or
materialistic urges to satisfy).

The opposite of financial freedom is *financial bondage.*
Those in financial bondage are enslaved—whether to loan
repayments, to debt, to discontentment, or to the siren
song of materialism. The Bible's many admonitions against
borrowing (Proverbs 22:7), co-signing (Proverbs 22:26), debt
(Psalm 37:21), and materialism (Luke 12:15) are clear calls
away from financial bondage and toward financial freedom.

For a more detailed look at the subject of financial bondage and its effects on ministry, refer to chapter 3.

Borrow

The word "borrow" means to receive something with either the implied or expressed intention of returning the
same thing or something of equal value. In this book, we
make every effort to distinguish between the meanings of
"borrow" and "debt." The act of borrowing, in and of itself,
is *not sinful or wrong* from a biblical perspective. However, because the returning of the item(s) borrowed takes
place in the uncertain future, borrowing is *risky.*

It's significant to note that the English word "borrow"
has its origins in ancient German terms that mean "to
save" or "to preserve." Since antiquity, the critical importance of repayment is integral to the concept of borrowing.

Repayment of what is borrowed is also at the core of biblical teaching: "The wicked borrow and do not repay, but the righteous give generously" (Psalm 37:21).

In this book we make a clear distinction between "debt" and "borrowing." *Borrowing* is the act of receiving with intent to repay. A condition of *debt* occurs when you owe more than you can pay (refer to our definition of "debt" for more details).

In one sense, the title of this book might be *The Borrow-Free Church.* Everyone—even those who believe in borrowing to fund ministry—agrees that ministries must not fall behind in their loan payments. But we're advocating what we believe to be a more biblical approach: that it's unwise and unnecessary for ministries to even *borrow* money. (We know that to some our non-borrowing approach may smack of fanaticism. We encourage you to read this entire book and let us present our case before you write us off.)

Lend

In a monetary sense, the word "lend" has a very clear-cut meaning: "to let out money for temporary use on condition that it be repaid with interest at an agreed time."[4] When you lend, the payment of interest is implicit in the arrangement; it's understood and automatic.

That's the definition we have in mind when we use the word "lend" in this book. And that's why Jesus' teaching about material things was so revolutionary, so hard to understand. He instructed His followers: "Love your enemies, do good to them, *and lend to them without expecting to get anything back.* Then your reward will be great, and you will be sons of the Most High . . ." (Luke 6:35, italics added).

Some of His followers must have murmured, "What could Jesus be talking about? The whole concept of 'lend' means that you get your money back with interest! He's saying to 'lend' without expecting to get *anything* back? Not even the *principal?* Is He out of His mind?" No, He wasn't crazy. Jesus was calling people to discipleship, to a complete commitment to follow Him. What He was really saying was more like: "Don't lend—*give*" (Luke 6:38).

Debt

Most people think of "debt" as a term covering any financial obligation. With this approach, making payments on a hospital bill or student loan is called "paying off debts."

But in this book, we use the word *debt* in a stricter, more traditional, more biblical sense. Simply put, debt is "a neglect or violation of duty."[5] Indebtedness is when your accounts are in arrears; when you are behind in your payments. In a biblical sense, debt refers to those who have broken their promise or vow and either will not or cannot repay what they owe.

Surety

This is an old-fashioned word, not generally used or well understood in today's world. A dictionary-style definition of surety is "agreeing to be responsible for someone else's debt" or "pledging more than you actually have as security for someone else's debt." An example of surety is co-signing another person's loan. In Old Testament times, a person who "became" or "stood" surety (for example, by co-signing) was said to be someone who "strikes hands in a pledge."

Most people don't take co-signing seriously. They don't seem to realize that when they co-sign, they *agree to actually pay* if the other person doesn't. If you co-sign, your agreement to pay is a legal contract, a solemn vow. If your cosigner cannot or will not pay, you *must* carry out your commitment—you are *obligated* to pay if the other cannot.

God takes a dim view of surety. According to Proverbs 11:15, the one who stands surety "will surely suffer." Proverbs 17:18 says that a person "lacking in judgment" (a fool) pledges his resources to cover another's financial obligations. Proverbs 22:26 commands, *"Do not* be a man who strikes hands in pledge or puts up security for debts" (emphasis added).

Biblically speaking, you can't determine whether co-signing is good by how it "turns out." You are in surety just by the *act* of co-signing; the outcome is irrelevant.

Usury

From both a biblical and a historical perspective, "usury" is the same as "interest." It was not until 1545 that English law redefined "usury" to mean "excessive interest."[6] Please note that *there is no biblical difference* between the two English words "interest" and "usury"; they are synonymous.[7] Both are used to translate the Hebrew word *nashek*.

The word *nashek* appears twenty-one times in the Old Testament. It comes from the root *nashak*—to strike with a sting, as would a venomous snake.[8] We find it interesting that the verbal root of *nashek* means "bite" or "sting" (an Aramaic cognate is used to describe a bee sting). The idea seems to be that interest can begin as a small thing (a bite or prick). Yet, over time, it can become a major source of pain and, ultimately, can be deadly. What a clear metaphor for the dangers of borrowing!

Consider these explanations of "usury" from several scholars:

- "Debt [borrowing] is a burden in any case, to a poor man especially; but debt is the heavier burden when to the original debt is added the constant payment of interest. Hence, not merely 'usury' in the modern sense of some excessive interest, but it is forbidden to claim or take any interest whatever from a Hebrew debtor." (S. H. Kellogg)[9]

- "Interest-free loans are well attested in ancient financial records, and laws against taking excessive interest are also known, but Israel is alone in totally prohibiting interest payments on loans. . . . These loans are essentially charitable." (G. J. Wenham)[10]

SCRIPTURE ABOUT BORROWING

The non-borrowing ministries we profile in this book all understand a vital biblical principle that is either unknown or ignored by many ministries: *The Bible cautions strongly against both borrowing and debt.* Yet many people either don't know that or are unwilling to acknowledge it. When we bring up the subject of ministries borrowing money, people often say, "But the Bible doesn't say borrowing is a *sin.*" Yes, it's true that borrowing is *not* the unpardonable sin. In fact, it's not a sin at all.

But the Bible *clearly says* that borrowing is *risky* and *unwise.* Scripture contains many cautions against borrowing and cites many negative consequences that can result from it. The Bible takes a stronger stand on debt: Scripture says that debt (nonpayment of obligations) is a *sin.* For examples of how strongly God warns against borrowing and condemns debt, refer to such passages as:

- Deuteronomy 15:1–9 (instructions about the Year of Jubilee)
- Deuteronomy 28:15–48 (indebtedness as a curse for unfaithfulness)
- 1 Samuel 22:2 (debt associated with stress and discontent)
- 2 Kings 6:5 (panic when a costly borrowed tool is lost)
- Psalm 37:21 (only the wicked borrow without repaying)
- Psalm 109:11 (David curses his enemies with debt)
- Proverbs 6:1–5 (do whatever is necessary to quickly get out of surety)
- Proverbs 17:18 (only a fool co-signs for what another has borrowed)
- Proverbs 22:7 (borrowers become slaves to lenders)
- Proverbs 22:26–27 (the danger of co-signing)
- Romans 13:8 (debts must not remain unpaid)

For a more detailed look at what the Bible says on the subjects of borrowing and debt, refer to chapter 4.

We conclude from God's Word that borrowed funds do not represent God's best plan, or His first choice, for ministry. The many non-borrowing ministries we talked to agree: God promises that He is willing and able to supply all the resources needed to accomplish His perfect will.

As non-borrowing ministries are often eager to describe, He supplies not through borrowing, but through the generous, joyous, and sacrificial giving of His people.

NOTES

1. Mel Sumrall, personal interview, 15 February 1995.

2. Mel Sumrall, personal interview, 27 May 1993.

3. "Miraculous Events Keep Churches Debt-Free," *Money Matters,* June 1995, 6–7; supplemented with information from John Thompson, personal interview, 27 July 1995.

4. *Webster's Third New International Dictionary* (Unabridged) (G. & C. Merriam Company, 1971), vol. 1.

5. *Webster's.*

6. "Usury," *Academic American Encyclopedia* (Grolier Electronic Publishing, 1995); accessed 15 April 1995 via Prodigy on-line service).

7. Francis Brown, S. R. Driver, and C. A. Briggs, *A Hebrew and English Lexicon of the Old Testament* (1907; reprint, Oxford: Clarendon, 1974), 675.

8. James Strong, *A Concise Dictionary of the Hebrew Bible* (1890; rpt. New York: Abingdon Press, 1967), 81.

9. S. H. Kellogg, *The Book of Leviticus,* 3d ed. (rpt. Minneapolis: Klock and Klock, 1978), 495.

10. G. J. Wenham, *The Book of Leviticus,* from *The New International Commentary on the Old Testament* (Grand Rapids: Eerdmans, 1979), 321–22.

CHAPTER 2

UNIQUE BENEFITS OF NON-BORROWING MINISTRY
The Spiritual and Practical Advantages of a Cash-Only Policy

In studying a wide range of ministries, we have seen that there are unique *spiritual* and *practical* benefits that are often possible only when a ministry operates without borrowed funds. We present and discuss many of these benefits in this chapter.

SPIRITUAL BENEFITS

As Christians, the quality of our spiritual lives is of vital importance. No matter how "successful" a ministry may appear from the outside, it is the inner depth of our spiritual walk that matters most to God. As God said to the prophet Samuel, "The Lord does not look at the things man looks at. Man looks at the outward appearance, but the Lord looks at the heart" (1 Samuel 16:7).

We have identified at least six key spiritual benefits that result from ministering on a non-borrowing basis, all of which we will examine in more detail throughout the book. We'll look at just a few in this chapter. A ministry that is "borrow-free":

- Depends more upon God
- Allows God to show His faithfulness

- Teaches the importance of giving
- Teaches sacrificial giving
- Teaches people to avoid surety
- Testifies to the world about the reality of the gospel

Not too long ago, Jim encountered a touching example of God's faithfulness and power in the life of a family in his church. As this book was being completed, Fellowship was in the process of raising the money to build a much-needed $1.4 million multipurpose facility. A few weeks after challenging his congregation to test the promise of Malachi 3, Jim received this letter from a member:

Dear Jim,

I want to let you know how God recently confirmed His faithfulness to our family. After hearing the presentation on the new church building, my wife and I felt led to give—over and above what we have already given—to the new building. Unable to squeeze more money out of our already stretched budget, we prayed that God would make additional funds available and we promised to give the whole amount to Him.

Five days later, my boss gave me a promotion and the largest raise of my career. Big money, several thousand dollars per year. Why do I tell you this? Because of the way God orchestrated the circumstances.

You see, our company's strict policies require all promotions to be completed by a certain date. And they had been. Some people got promoted, but I wasn't among them. In the past, if you got passed over at promotion time, you had to wait until the next year. So I had resigned myself to wait until next year.

Well, that didn't happen. I got the promotion and the biggest raise of my career. My wife and I decided that the entire amount —the gross—will now go monthly toward the new building.

It's exciting to see that God hasn't given up on me yet, but has chosen to work through me. And it's not from any effort I put out; He has simply provided. I can't wait to see what else He's going to do. It's fantastic to be a part of God's will.

Believing He will do even greater things,
A fellow worker in Christ

Remember this: Whoever sows sparingly will also reap sparingly, and whoever sows generously will also reap generously. Each man should give what he has decided in his heart to give, not reluctantly or under compulsion, for God loves a cheerful giver. And God is able to make all grace abound to you, so that in all things at all times, having all that you need, you will abound in every good work. (2 Corinthians 9:6-8)

Teaches Sacrificial Giving

Paul encouraged the church at Corinth to give sacrificially with this testimony of giving from Macedonia:

> And now, brothers, we want you to know about the grace that God has given the Macedonian churches. Out of the most severe trial, their overflowing joy and their extreme poverty welled up in rich generosity. For I testify that they gave as much as they were able, and even beyond their ability. Entirely on their own, they urgently pleaded with us for the privilege of sharing in this service to the saints. And they did not do as we expected, but they gave themselves first to the Lord and then to us in keeping with God's will. (2 Corinthians 8:1-5)

One church that has seen the miracle of sacrificial giving is First Baptist Church of Atlanta. In 1981 Pastor Charles Stanley challenged his congregation to raise $2.85 million to purchase some much-needed property—without borrowing.

The congregation responded warmly, but as months passed it began to appear that the deadline for raising the money would pass with only $125,000 being collected. Stanley admits he was tempted to borrow the money. "I really struggled with what we should do," he said. "We really needed that property for our ministry, so maybe we should go ahead and borrow the rest. I was wrestling in my heart, my own faith was being challenged. But it came to me clearly that God would provide the money."[1]

What happened next was reported a few weeks later in the Atlanta *Journal:*

> On Sunday, February 22, eight days before the $2.85 million was due, only $125,000 had been given. Following the 8 A.M. service, a young couple came forward and told Stanley

that God had told them to give the church their jewelry. They told the minister they had been robbed several weeks earlier and this was all they had left to give.

Stanley was temporarily stunned by their offer. "I don't want to take it unless you feel that the Lord really wants you to give it," he finally told them.

The husband said they had prayed about it and knew it was right. He gave a diamond wedding band.

During the 11 A.M. worship service, Stanley told the congregation of the couple's gift, likening it to the scripture about the people of Israel bringing their gold and silver to the Temple.

At the close of that service, Stanley says, people walked to the altar for more than 45 minutes, giving jewelry, money, and titles to automobiles, motorcycles and boats.

"All manner of material wealth was brought to be used by God," Stanley says. "The people came out of a heart of love, sacrificing items of tremendous value to them that they might know more of God. They were obeying the scriptures."

"God provided . . . ," says Stanley, as contributions continued to come in [until they] had the rest of the money.[2]

Teaches People to Avoid Surety

Earlier in this chapter we discussed the practice of *surety*, in which one contractually commits to be responsible for another's financial obligation if the other cannot pay. The Scripture is clear that only fools go into surety for another (Proverbs 22:26–27).

Yet throughout America, ministry leaders are signing loan documents that personally obligate them in the event the ministry cannot pay. In most cases this is surety, and it sets a poor example in a culture that suffers from an addiction to borrowing.

If a ministry leader has the resources to personally pay off the entire loan amount if the ministry defaults, that ministry leader may not technically have become surety for the church. However, due to the inherent risks of borrowing and the uncertainty of the future, one's finances may be fully adequate today yet completely inadequate tomorrow.

Tragically, the number of elders, deacons, trustees, and even church members who are being required by ministry creditors to pay for ministry indebtedness is increasing.

In contrast, a non-borrowing ministry obligates no one. The pay-as-you-go, live-within-your-means practice of a balanced, non-borrowing ministry does not presume on the future and puts no one's personal finances at risk. Ministry leaders who live by and promote the non-borrowing concept are correctly teaching their congregations to heed the strong scriptural cautions against surety.

Testifies to the World About the Reality of the Gospel
Christians are instructed to be lights in a dark world (Philippians 2:15). We are supposed to make a difference, especially to the spiritually lost. God, speaking through the apostle Peter, has given us a clear mission:

> But you are a chosen people, a royal priesthood, a holy nation, a people belonging to God, that you may declare the praises of him who called you out of darkness into his wonderful light. Live such good lives among the pagans that, though they accuse you of doing wrong, they may see your good deeds and glorify God on the day he visits us. (1 Peter 2:9, 12)

Throughout this book, we present examples of how non-borrowing ministries are having a powerful and godly effect on the world around them. Non-borrowing ministries are often outstanding examples of Christlike community service. And the pastors and leaders of those ministries will gladly tell you that they couldn't have the effect they do if they weren't non-borrowing.

Just one example of a non-borrowing ministry with an impact for God is Prince Avenue Baptist Church of Athens, Georgia. Prince Avenue has been "borrow-free" since the early seventies. Since then the congregation has used the money they would have spent on loans and interest to influence both their community and the world. Among a few of the church's ministries are:

- A crisis pregnancy center
- Korean and Hispanic ministries
- Support for an ever-increasing number of foreign missions

- A Christian radio station
- A K-12 Christian school

The Prince Avenue congregation has also shown the unbelieving world how God can fund building programs. Since 1980 the church has seen God provide several buildings without borrowing:

- 1980—$1.4 million educational building
- 1991—$760,000 family life center
- 1994—$1.4 million sanctuary renovation

In a non-borrowing ministry, God provides through the sacrificial giving of His people. Banks, bonds, and loans do not play a part. As the world sees God's people doing God's work with God's methods, the "pagans" will "see [our] good deeds" and be drawn to Christ.

For detailed information about what the Bible says about funding ministry, refer to chapter 4.

PRACTICAL BENEFITS

Popular opinion to the contrary, non-borrowing ministry makes sense, even from a practical perspective. Pastor John Thompson of Grace Bible Fellowship said, "We are a debt-free ministry for *philosophical* rather than *pragmatic* reasons. However, there are many practical reasons why it makes sense to have a debt-free ministry."[3]

We have identified at least seven important practical benefits that result from ministering on a non-borrowing basis. A non-borrowing mind-set:

- Helps prevent a focus on fund-raising
- Allows interest funds to be invested for eternity
- Helps promote Christian unity
- Sets a financial example for believers
- Helps guard a ministry from hard economic times

- Encourages members' active involvement
- Stimulates ministry creativity and innovation

Helps Prevent a Focus on Fund-Raising

A non-borrowing ministry does not need to pressure people to meet looming loan-payment deadlines. Non-borrowing ministries simply present the ministry need, then trust God to provide through the generous giving of His people.

In contrast, when ministries are burdened with loan repayments or debt, they are often forced to develop a constant fund-raising focus. Even a ministry that has traditionally had a balanced approach to fund-raising can find itself in terrible straits when its leaders succumb to the lure of easy, immediate expansion with borrowed funds.

Consider the case of a formerly growing church in a small southwestern city. Like many ministries, this church gambled on the strength of its future growth and borrowed a large amount of money for a new building. However, as is all too often the case, things didn't quite work out as the congregation had hoped. Unable to make the loan payments, the church hired a professional fund-raiser.

Among the fund-raiser's recommendations was that the church should send a letter to every staff member and Sunday-school teacher, *requiring* them to return a signed pledge card. Those who did not return the signed pledge would be *prohibited* from teaching or serving in the church in any official capacity! Unable to deal with the overwhelming financial pressure, staff members are resigning, church members are leaving, and worship attendance is declining.

Look closely at 1 Corinthians 16:1–2. Paul says,

> Now about the collection for God's people: Do what I told the Galatian churches to do. On the first day of every week, each one of you should set aside a sum of money in keeping with his income, saving it up, so that when I come no collections will have to be made.

Paul clearly states that he does not want fund-raising to interfere with his ministry; he wants collections to be completed before he arrives. Throughout his ministry, Paul was extremely careful to separate himself from any hint of materialism—even to the point of denying himself what he considered to be the right of every gospel minister: to earn his living from the gospel (1 Corinthians 9:7–18). Paul was concerned about the message of the gospel being hindered by the appearance of materialism (v. 12).

Paul's passion was that the gospel be offered without charge to anyone (v. 18). How different that is from the fund-raising pressure we often see exerted by ministries that are burdened with the need to repay loans.

Allows Interest Funds to Be Invested for Eternity

Across America, non-borrowing ministries are employing a wide range of creative approaches to ministry. The entire world has felt the impact since the 6,000-member Frazier Memorial United Methodist Church of Montgomery, Alabama, paid off its last loan in 1993. Since then the church has redirected *all the money* that was formerly going toward loan repayment into ministry—a total of $750,000 annually! With those funds, Frazier Memorial has begun two massive outreach projects:

- *Project Apostle* has greatly expanded both the church's foreign and home missions efforts. For example, in a recent home missions project, the church helped sponsor three thousand men from the Montgomery area to attend a Promise Keepers Conference.

- *Project Judea* is designed to help Frazier Memorial reach its community for Christ. For example, the church has used some of the Project Judea funds to acquire a low-power television license and broadcasting equipment. Frazier Memorial is now producing television programming for its own broadcasts, for the local cable company, and for overseas distribution. As a result, additional thousands are being reached with the gospel.

Project Apostle and Project Judea, made possible only by Frazier Memorial's non-borrowing commitment, have been so successful that the entire congregation recently voted to remain permanently "borrow-free." As of summer 1995, the church was planning to build a $2.3 million educational building and community outreach center—with *no borrowing*. According to Frazier Memorial's church administrator, Rusty Taylor, "Our people are so thrilled with what we see happening as a result of being out of debt we will never go back to borrowing."[4]

Benevolence is another area of ministry that is most effectively performed when a ministry is debt-free. Consider these compelling words written by the apostle John near the end of his life:

> If anyone has material possessions and sees his brother in need but has no pity on him, how can the love of God be in him? Dear children, let us not love with words or tongue but with actions and in truth. (1 John 3:17–18)

Some churches are awakening to the mandate to care financially for fellow believers who are truly in need. But as the family structure and the national work ethic decline, the needs grow greater each year.

Although ministry needs are increasing, charitable giving is down.[5] As a result, many churches are forced to cut staff. And if those staff personnel were involved with teaching, leading, counseling, and helping, the vital "high-touch" aspect of Christian ministry can suffer. When faced with the question "Do we cut staff or do we cut back on our loan payments?" staff is almost invariably the first to go.

Nothing guarantees that a ministry will never need to cut its staff. And a church with unnecessary personnel *should* reduce its "headcount" to a level that is appropriate to the ministry's actual needs. But a non-borrowing church can invest more aggressively in staff ministry because there is less demanding competition for funds.

Helps Promote Christian Unity

Borrowing money is among the most potentially divisive catalysts in the American church. Ministries across the nation are contending, dividing, splitting, and even dissolving over borrowed money and the indebtedness that too often follows.

In fact, one of the primary reasons we have written this book is to help ministries (and their testimonies) survive—and even thrive. Paul said in 1 Corinthians 1:10, "I appeal to you, brothers, in the name of our Lord Jesus Christ, that all of you agree with one another so that there may be no divisions among you and that you may be perfectly united in mind and thought." Non-borrowing ministries around the country repeatedly tell inspiring stories of unity and harmony, which, they assert, are a direct result of their non-borrowing philosophy.

One example of a unity-building ministry experience is when a congregation builds its own building. For example, both Circle Community Church of Orlando and Spirit Lake Baptist Church of Spirit Lake, Idaho, have built borrow-free buildings with the labor of their own congregations. Circle's 300-seat auditorium was completed in the late 1980s; Spirit Lake's 250-seat sanctuary was completed in late 1995. Both churches have joyous memories of the unity their congregations experienced as everyone worked together to build.

Kim Alexander, pastor of Spirit Lake Baptist, said, "It was just like in Nehemiah, where the people had a mind to work—and they worked together," referring to how the returning Jewish exiles labored in harmony to rebuild Jerusalem's walls under Nehemiah's leadership in 445 B.C.[6]

"You definitely get a bonding when people pull together to build," noted Jim Sowers, Spirit Lake Baptist's only deacon. "When we're working together, we get to know each other—what we're doing, where we're hurting, and so forth."[7]

Sets a Financial Example for Believers

American families are struggling economically. Despite the fact that Americans enjoy the world's highest standard of living, more and more American Christians are feeling financially challenged. The pain, however, is usually not from starvation. More often it's from overindulgence. Americans have overindulged themselves with a high-fat diet of easy credit.

Non-borrowing ministries, operating by faith as God supplies and living within their means, can be a shining light of example to Christian families, many of which have come to believe that credit is a necessity and borrowing is inevitable. A non-borrowing ministry can serve as an excellent role model for personal and family financial teaching.

It's vitally important that ministry leaders have both their ministry finances and their personal finances well in order. The Bible is clear on this point. Paul told Timothy that elders and deacons must be good managers of their households and families (1 Timothy 3:4, 5, 12). James cautions that not many should be teachers, because they will be held to a higher standard (James 3:1).

This is not to say that a ministry leader should be disqualified if he owes money. However, we believe that ministry leaders are most financially effective for God when they are committed to being "borrow-free" and are moving on a non-borrowing track as rapidly as possible.

When the leaders of an open, non-borrowing ministry have their personal finances in order, people have the financial models they need. And they can confidently bring their financial problems to those leaders.

Helps Guard a Ministry from Hard Economic Times

Proverbs 22:27 warns about what can happen when loans are not repaid: "If you lack the means to pay, your very bed will be snatched from under you." And in economic downturns around the country, ministries are indeed having their very "beds" taken right out from under them.

The reason for this fragile state of affairs is, once again, too much borrowing. The more a family or ministry borrows, the more it puts itself at risk. In a community where leveraged (loan-financed) churches are supported by leveraged families who work for leveraged companies, even a slight "blip" in the local economy can put both families and churches at financial risk.

An unfortunate example of this scenario occurred some years ago in Texas during the "oil bust." In a declining petroleum market, large portions of the Lone Star State were confronted with failing companies, rising unemployment, plummeting real estate prices, and unpaid loans. As their loans became debts, many families virtually stopped giving to their churches, which, in turn, had been built and were sustained by loans. Many Texas churches were forced into bankruptcy as both attendance and giving declined sharply. Debt-free churches could have been in a unique position to minister to those who were hurting financially, but many churches were removed from the picture just when they could have had the greatest opportunity for ministry and a testimony for the Lord.

However, economic hard times for ministries can result from other factors as well. What if an especially well-loved pastor leaves and many people follow him to his new ministry or simply drift away in his absence? What if an exciting new church starts in the area and draws away a large number of people? What if a nationwide economic downturn occurs, as some experts speculate? Situations such as these can really throw a monkey wrench into the gears of church growth plans—especially those that are financed by borrowing.

Because a non-borrowing ministry is not enslaved to a loan repayment schedule, it is more flexible and much more able to weather life's economic storms. Please don't think we're saying that non-borrowing ministries are perfect or trouble-free. Far from it. But a non-borrowing ministry is much more likely to survive hard economic times than a ministry burdened with loans.

Encourages Members' Active Involvement

Because non-borrowing ministry depends heavily on everyone's active contribution, churches and ministries consistently report that non-borrowing ministry yields a high level of personal involvement.

Writing in Romans 12:4–8 and 1 Corinthians 12:12–27, Paul presents a beautiful and evocative illustration of how all believers are parts of one body—the body of Christ. And

God has given gifts, abilities, and resources for ministry to everyone who is born again. In these passages, Paul stresses the importance of all Christians sharing their ministry gifts and abilities to the fullest.

When you minister without borrowing, you usually can't simply go out and buy everything you need. Thus people are more compelled to become involved, knowing that their contribution truly matters. And *involvement* is exactly what non-borrowing ministries are experiencing.

In the course of writing this book, we talked with and visited non-borrowing churches from coast to coast. We found that the leaders of non-borrowing ministries almost unanimously cite the energetic commitment of their people as a key factor of their ability to minister without borrowing. Referring to the way in which the congregation of Spirit Lake Baptist Church built its new auditorium, Pastor Kim Alexander said, "Our building project has drawn people together in fellowship and then helped build them up in spiritual maturity."[8]

Stimulates Ministry Creativity and Innovation

When a ministry has a non-borrowing commitment, people are challenged in several significant ways. They are challenged to give, to be involved, and sometimes to sacrifice.

Another way that people are challenged in a non-borrowing ministry is in the area of creativity. After all, the non-borrowing ministry can't call the bank and get a line-of-credit extension. Because the ministry depends upon God to work through people, people are often stretched creatively when trying to fund ministry and accomplish ministry goals.

How great it is to serve an inspiring and creative God! He stands ready to help and inspire us in our efforts to fund and accomplish His ministry. When describing to the prophet Jeremiah how He would minister to Israel, God encouraged the prophet with these words: "Call to me and I will answer you and tell you great and unsearchable things you do not know" (Jeremiah 33:3). In non-borrowing churches across America, God is inspiring His people to find new and exciting ministry methods.

A church that doesn't lack for innovative fund-raising ideas is First Baptist Church of Orlando, Florida. With ten thousand members and nearly five thousand in attendance on any given Sunday, First Baptist is one of America's largest congregations. According to Bill Silkman, the church's business administrator, its $42 million campus is currently a non-borrowing facility.[9]

In January 1993, First Baptist was close to completing a three-year fund-raising effort to build a $5.1 million fellowship hall without borrowing. After Pastor Jim Henry delivered an inspiring sermon on the parable of the talents (Matthew 25), one-dollar bills were passed out to anyone who was interested in investing and "growing" God's resources. Nearly $4,500 was distributed in this way, and church members began to use ingenuity, hard work, and prayer to multiply the Lord's money.

Silkman described a few of the projects that people undertook:

- Two members had their dollar bills signed by celebrities; they then had the bills silently auctioned to the highest bidder. One man had his dollar signed by Orlando Magic basketball star Shaquille O'Neal; a woman had her bill signed by former U.S. president George Bush.

- Some children made cassette tapes of Bible stories and songs and sold the tapes.

- Other children bought shoe polish and earned money shining shoes.

- Some students bought gasoline for lawnmowers and donated their mowing income.

- Several members bought price stickers, held garage sales, and donated the proceeds.

- One person bought a newspaper, clipped the coupons, bought groceries, and donated the savings.

- One member used his dollar to make a long distance call that enabled him to save money on a large purchase; he donated the savings.
- Another individual used her dollar to place a real-estate ad in the newspaper. She donated the entire commission when the property sold.

When the increase from what became known as the "Jesus Dollars" was returned to the church in March 1993, the people had invested just two months in completing their projects. When the gifts were finally added up, the church found that its $4,500 "Jesus Dollars" had grown by a factor of more than twenty—to $97,500![10]

NOTES

1. Billie Cheney Speed, "Contributions Keep Coming at Atlanta's First Baptist," *Atlanta Journal,* 14 March 1981.
2. Ibid.
3. John Thompson, personal interview, 27 July 1995.
4. Rusty Taylor, personal interview, 28 July 1995.
5. Helen Lee, "Churches Battle Downward Donations," *Christianity Today,* 24 April 1995; accessed via America Online.
6. Kim Alexander, personal interview, 9 April 1995.
7. Jim Sowers, personal interview, 9 April 1995.
8. Kim Alexander, personal interview, 9 April 1995.
9. Bill Silkman, personal interview, 28 July 1995.
10. Bill Silkman, "A Faithful Journey," *NACBA Ledger,* April-June 1993, 12–13.

"We ran out of money right after we built the pulpit."

CHAPTER 3

THE CHURCH IN BONDAGE
Facing the Challenges of Debt-Burdened Ministry

As we have previously noted, it's not a sin to borrow money. But it is risky—unnecessarily so. And if your borrowing leads to surety or indebtedness, you'll find yourself in violation of important biblical financial principles. This chapter tells the unfortunate stories of churches and ministries that took the risk, borrowed to fund ministry, and have been hampered or even destroyed by borrowing and debt.

In the nineteenth century, the *Boston Recorder* championed the cause of the antigambling movement. To drive home the seriousness of the gambling problem, the *Recorder* "covered particular people who gambled and lost everything. They gave face to the issue."[1]

Today many ministries are "gambling" that their financial situations will not change before they can repay their loans. They are "gambling" that they can disregard scriptural cautions and not suffer the consequences.

Our goal in this chapter is to "give face" to the issue of ministry borrowing. In so doing, our prayer is that Christian ministries will wake up to the dangers of borrowing and do whatever they can to avoid it.

This was a difficult chapter to write. Apart from the negative and discouraging aspects of hindered and destroyed
ministry, it was hard just to get information.

In "borrow-free" and debt-free ministries, we found that
people are often eager to tell about the way God is working
in their lives. In sharp contrast, those who are (or were)
involved in loan-burdened ministries are often reluctant to
discuss their situations. Several people (including some
pastors) would not return our phone calls. Others feared
for their jobs, requiring that we pledge not to reveal any
details about their ministries. Some forbade us to tell their
stories at all, also for fear of reprisals.

Even more so than non-borrowing ministries, loan-funded
ministries can be found throughout America. Like non-
borrowing ministries, loan-funded ministries come in all
sizes and denominations. That's because in America,
Christian ministry is most often funded by borrowing. It's
the normal thing to do.

However, the "normal" thing for Americans is contrary
to God's ministry principles. And when ministries fail to
conform to God's principles, they often reap unpleasant
consequences.

THE HEARTACHE OF LOAN-FUNDED MINISTRY

Many people don't want to talk about ministry borrowing. The issue too often separates Christians, and sometimes it splits entire congregations. Yet few Christians
(even few theologians) have carefully studied this volatile
subject in the light of Scripture.

Like the stories of non-borrowing churches, there are
many borrowing stories to tell, and we've tried to incorporate as many as possible into this book. After much debate,
we decided to open this chapter with the profiles of only
three loan-burdened churches. We have had to change the
names and pertinent details of several of these ministries
to disguise the situations of those who requested anonymity.
Unfortunately, these ministries represent but the tip of a
very large iceberg:

- The Growing Church
- The Large Church
- The Small Church

Ministry Profile 1—The Growing Church
In the 1960s, a group of twenty-eight Christians met in a living room to start a church. Within a few years that church, which was located on the outskirts of a large town, had grown to more than three thousand members. Its Sunday school was hailed as one of the hundred largest and fastest growing in America. Yet today that church is but a memory—destroyed by runaway borrowing and debt.

The ministry began with all the right ingredients for rapid growth—a dynamic young pastor, a group of committed believers, and a fast-growing suburban area in need of a good church. At first things went well. God provided land in an ideal location with a small but adequate building. The ministry grew rapidly.

However, as the church grew, so did the pastor's desires. Before long there was talk of a larger building, more land, and a Christian school. All of it was to be financed with borrowed funds. The congregation sold its original property at less than its full value (as is often the case with church property). The ministry purchased a much larger tract of land and erected an elaborate new building.

The church's growth was financed with a combination of bonds and conventional loans. Gradually the debt climbed to several million dollars.

After a time, the momentum of borrowed funding ground to a halt. The church's expenses began to exceed its income, and the congregation once again turned to borrowing. Ultimately the ministry's loan payments exceeded its ability to repay. Attendance declined, and it was soon obvious that the ministry was dying.

It took several excruciating years before the final scene was played out. The church had destroyed itself with debt. To this day, many of the ministry's creditors have never been repaid. When we interviewed the son of the church's original pastor, he was reluctant to discuss the death of what had once been one of America's leading churches. "We try not to talk about it," he said.

Ministry Profile 2—The Large Church

A large West-Coast church knows firsthand the misery of financial bondage. Several years ago the congregation raised half of the money for a building program that was projected to cost in excess of $10 million. They planned to sell bonds to finance the remaining half.

However, through a series of unforeseen and unfortunate circumstances, the cost of the new building gradually ballooned to nearly twice its original projection. This century-old church, which had never before borrowed money, ultimately found itself strapped with a financial obligation of more than $15 million. Then, six months after moving into the new building, the dynamic senior pastor left the church for another position.

Attendance declined. Giving also dropped off, and soon the church was struggling to make ends meet. In an effort to pay back the bonds and reduce its financial burden, the church approached a local bank and was able to refinance the debt at a lower interest rate. But the new financing arrangements dictated that one-fourth of the church's income had to go toward debt service. The ministry continued to struggle financially, and it wasn't long before the church's leaders were forced to ask the bank for an extension on one of their loan payments. The bank agreed, but only if the church would *cut nearly half a million dollars* out of the next year's operating budget. Bank officials even required the church to submit a budget draft, from which the bank "suggested" which cuts to make!

The ministry had little choice but to agree to the bank's demands. As a result, a significant number of personnel were laid off and every department of the church was required to drastically cut expenses.

Church leaders are now forced to constantly keep the great financial needs in front of the people. At last report, tensions were running high and members were leaving. But perhaps most tragically, the church finds itself in the unfortunate position of not being able to respond to genuine ministry opportunities in the way it would like to. As one staff member observed with regret, "It's tough when the bank begins dictating ministry, and that's what's happening. I just hope other churches can learn from our mistake."

Ministry Profile 3—The Small Church

Several years ago Jim received a call from an associate pastor who was on staff at a small church. He was concerned about the financial health of his 250-member church and was looking for advice. To pay for a new building, the congregation had issued bonds and raised $750,000. However, neither growth nor giving increased as expected. The church was struggling just to survive.

At that time 40 percent of the ministry's weekly income was going toward its debt. "There are many weeks when I don't get paid," the associate pastor confessed. "And to make matters worse, some of the wealthier members have snatched up the best bonds and are trying to use them to control the church. All we do anymore is fight over money."

Jim prayed with him and encouraged him not to stop trying to teach biblical financial principles. Jim also promised to call and encourage the church's senior pastor. He called repeatedly, leaving many messages. Yet despite frequent promises of a call back, Jim never heard from the senior pastor.

Recently Jim grew curious about the church's situation and called the associate pastor for an update. Much to Jim's delight, the associate pastor was once again excited about the work of the ministry. However, he was no longer on staff at the loan-burdened church—he had taken a job at a gas station while planting a new, non-borrowing ministry.

Unfortunately, his former church was continuing down the same self-destructive path. After the church's earlier financial crisis was averted due to falling interest rates, the ministry borrowed an additional $150,000. Soon the church was once again unable to make its payments. So the congregation hired a fund-raising consultant who helped raise an additional $100,000—but charged them $20,000 to do it! At last report, church leaders were exerting tremendous pressure on their people to give.

SPIRITUAL PROBLEMS ASSOCIATED
WITH MINISTRY BORROWING

Like a lighthouse brightly shining forth in a foggy night, the Bible warns repeatedly against borrowing money. That's because borrowing is often an indicator of subtle yet powerful spiritual problems at work. This section discusses three of the spiritual problems that are too often associated with ministry borrowing:

- Financial bondage
- Circumventing God's will
- Using human instead of divine methods

Financial Bondage

Another way to describe this problem is *loss of freedom*. In Proverbs 22:7, the Bible refers to it as *enslavement*.

Proverbs 22:7 is one of the Bible's strongest cautions regarding the risks of borrowing: "The rich rule over the poor, and the borrower is servant to the lender." This verse is presented in Scripture toward the end of a long collection of Solomon's wisdom on a wide variety of practical subjects. Much of his advice is presented in the form of cause and effect. Proverbs 22:7 is a perfect example: If you sow borrowing, you will harvest slavery.

The Hebrew word for "borrow" used in Proverbs 10:1– 22:16 is *lawa*. It comes from a root word that means "to twine, to twist together . . . to unite, or to join."[2] This word is used elsewhere in Scripture to describe a wife joining herself to her husband (Genesis 29:34) and a man joining himself to the Lord (Isaiah 56:3). Inherent in both of these examples is the idea of joining yourself to someone or something that will have control or authority over you.

In much the same way, a borrower joins himself to a lender in a slave/master relationship. A borrower cannot make even the smallest financial decision without being forced to ask himself, "How will this decision affect my ability to repay what I owe?" And if the amount borrowed becomes a debt (cannot be repaid), the lender may actually take control of the debtor and his resources and literally "rule" over him. As one Old Testament commentary puts it, "the contracting of debt brings with it a slavish relation of dependence on the lender."[3] We have already presented examples of how this is happening in American ministries.

Perhaps commentator Otto Zocklear said it most succinctly: "Indebtedness always destroys freedom."[4]

Circumventing God's Will

The Bible teaches that God is sovereign. He has everything in the universe under His benevolent control. However, people also have choices, and they *can* do things that are contrary to God's principles and desires. In the materialistic American culture, the abuse of easy credit is one of the most deceptive ways to run away from and fight against God's direction in the lives of Christians.

Borrowing can be a subversive tool that reaches outside God's sovereign, unseen will and artificially manufactures that which God has purposefully kept from His people. Ron Blue observes that "debt is almost blasphemous when we use it and deny God an opportunity to work."[5]

If your ministry lacks vital resources, you should ask God, "Why aren't our people supporting this need with their giving?" God has promised to supply our needs (Philippians 4:19), and He does so through the generous, joyful, and sacrificial giving of His people (Philippians 4:14–18). Borrowing is usually *not* the most effective way to acquire necessary resources. It's too often a way to make an "end run" around God's will.

Using Human Instead of Divine Methods

As we have previously stated, borrowing is a worldly approach to ministry, not a divine one. One of the dangers of borrowing is that it enables ministries to appear "successful" beyond the actual means God has entrusted to them. According to Job 31:24–28, God's people must not put their trust in wealth or in the gods of this world. When you fund ministry through borrowing, your ministry "success" is not measured by how generously people give, but by how much the bank is willing to lend.

Too many ministries and individual Christians are handling their finances according to the world's principles. The concepts of borrowing and leverage are straight from Wall Street, not from the pages of God's Word. The Bible, rather than Harvard Business School, ought to be the Christian's first source of guidance and direction when funding ministry.

To a greater or lesser extent, every ministry that borrows must deal with these problems. However, by trusting God to supply instead of borrowing, ministries can usually avoid financial bondage. And when a ministry refuses to borrow money, it is heeding the cautions of God's Word and relying solely on God's funding methods.

MINISTRY DISADVANTAGES
ASSOCIATED WITH BORROWING

Not only does borrowing often involve spiritual problems, but it can burden a ministry with distinct disadvantages. These disadvantages are not mere inconveniences. Rather, they are serious barriers to ministry effectiveness. In some cases, these disadvantages overwhelm a ministry.

We have identified at least five of these borrowing disadvantages. When it borrows, a ministry risks:

- Becoming the slave of a lending institution
- Becoming a slave to big givers
- Becoming trapped by financial pressure
- Becoming mired in an endless cycle of borrowing
- Losing flexibility to respond to ministry opportunities

All these disadvantages are symptoms of financial bondage. Let's examine them in more detail.

Becoming the Slave of a Lending Institution
According to Proverbs 22:7, those who borrow become the slaves of their lenders—*whether or not* their borrowing leads to indebtedness (more on this later). When you bor-

row, the issue is not *if* you're in slavery, but what kind of taskmaster you must serve. Some lenders are relatively kind taskmasters who demand little. Others are harsh and exacting, requiring much, regardless of how little you have.

In the case of the large church (ministry profile 2), the church fell behind in its payments, and the bank (whose officers are not Christians) now oversees the ministry efforts. It has been said that whenever you borrow, you take on a business partner. But do Christian ministries really want banks as their ministry partners?

Church management consultant David Pollock warns, "When your church borrows, you automatically reorder all of its priorities. Debt becomes an 800-pound gorilla that sits on the platform of the church and demands to be fed every week. Because of the laws in this country, you have to pay the debt as your first and foremost priority."[6]

Becoming a Slave to Big Givers

When a ministry borrows, its supporters become pressured to give because the financial obligation must be met. And when the pressure is on, ministry leaders too often look to the ministry's "big givers" for extra help. Several pastors of loan-funded ministries told us they were tempted to give preferential treatment to big contributors.

The apostle Paul, paraphrasing Job 41:11, says in Romans 11:35, "Who has ever given to God, that God should repay him?" God is obliged to no one, and control over Christ's body cannot be bought. However, the materialistic control that comes from being a lender sometimes goes to people's heads. How much better to "lend" freely, expecting nothing in return—neither profit nor control (Luke 6:35).

Becoming Trapped by Financial Pressure

In the course of our research for this book, we learned that financial pressure and worry are constant afflictions in many loan-funded ministries. People told us of tension, anxiety, factions, and unrest within congregations. Others told us that the distractions associated with repaying loans invaded their personal devotional times, making it difficult to effectively read the Bible or pray.

These problems can be largely avoided by trusting God's provision instead of borrowing. If God *doesn't* provide for ministry needs through the generous giving of His people, *He has good reasons* for not doing so—and you can trust Him for the outcome. Or if God wants people to give and they refuse to, borrowing money instead is short-circuiting God's leading in their lives.

One of the most painful disadvantages of ministry borrowing is the emotional and spiritual impact it can have on individual Christians. Jim tells the heartbreaking story of a Missouri pastor's wife who wrote to him after hearing him speak on the subject of ministry borrowing. The church was burdened with high loan payments from a building project that had been completed shortly before the pastor and his family were called to the church. She wrote:

> The church has repeatedly failed to meet its financial obligations to us. Sometimes my husband doesn't get paid his full salary. Twice he didn't get paid at all. As a result, I have been forced to work outside the home, even though we agreed I would quit when our children were born.
>
> I can't begin to tell you how often my husband and I fight over money. There never seems to be enough to pay the bills. Each month I find myself becoming more bitter with the church and, I'm ashamed to say, with God. I know this is wrong, but I can't seem to do anything about it.
>
> My husband feels it would be inappropriate to speak with the deacons about our situation. He thinks it is just a matter of time until the church grows and everything will be all right. Meanwhile, our children go without new shoes and proper dental care, and I become more disgusted every week. I used to love to go to church and worship. Now it's all I can do to make myself go. Please pray for us.

Becoming Mired in an Endless Cycle of Borrowing

Contrary to what many believe, you can't borrow your way out of debt. Borrowing too often becomes financial quicksand—once you get caught, it's difficult to break free. The perceived "need" to borrow sometimes becomes a runaway train, with momentum of its own.

The small church (ministry profile 3) responded like too many indebted families do when they secure a bill consolidation loan: It just went right back to borrowing. After the pressure eased, the leaders failed to recognize their mistake and returned to the same methods that created the problems.

Losing Flexibility to Respond to Ministry Opportunities

When a ministry is repaying loans at interest, it's difficult to respond to unforeseen ministry needs. In the course of our research, we discovered this to be one of the most frequently cited reasons that ministries pay off their loans and adopt a non-borrowing policy.

An example of how a flexible, "borrow-free" ministry can respond to unexpected needs is Fellowship Bible Church in Dalton, Georgia. During the Romanian revolution of December 1989, dictator Nicolae Ceausescu was driven out of power and the entire country was suddenly open to the gospel. At that time, Fellowship supported a missionary in Romania. This missionary worked with a group known as "The Lord's Army," an evangelical branch of the Romanian Orthodox Church.

Rejoicing in the country's new-found post-revolutionary freedom, the missionary invited Jim and his wife to conduct several Bible-based seminars in Romania. Jim felt it was a wonderful opportunity to teach the Bible and help fulfill the Great Commission.

The Windowless Church. While he was in Romania, Jim visited one particular church that he could not get out of his mind. It was nothing more than a small house, long and narrow with narrow, makeshift benches serving as pews. People were crammed tighter into that building than any place he had ever seen. Jim also noticed that all the windowpanes were missing, which he thought unusual because of the fairly cold climate.

When Jim asked about the missing windowpanes, he was told that they had been removed so people could stand outside and still hear what was being said inside. And sure enough, before the three-hour service was over, heads filled every window opening. The people were starving for God's Word.

Upon his return to the United States, Jim told the story of the windowless church to his fellow elders and Fellowship's deacons. As they listened to Jim speak, the Holy Spirit broke their hearts. They began to ask what role they could play in Romania's spiritual revolution. The vision of helping Romania began to sweep through the church.

Redirecting Funds for God's Glory. If Fellowship had been burdened with loan payments, the church would have been able to do very little. The ministry lived on a careful budget, and help for Romania had never been envisioned when that budget was designed. But the church had been gradually accumulating a building fund, and the congregation decided to send half of its building fund to the windowless Romanian church. Fellowship's leaders had learned that with *only one-half* of their building fund, the Romanians could build an entire new church that would meet their needs for years to come.

Fellowship's congregation also decided to contribute some additional building-fund money to supply the Romanian church with something else that it lacked completely —hymnals. Hymnals are extremely important to Romanians, who dearly love singing and poetry. So Fellowship's Romanian missionary mailed a set of hand-typed Romanian worship songs to Dalton. The church had the songs typeset, printed, and bound. Soon 5,000 Romanian worship hymnals were shipped to Romania. Today those hymnals are being used for God's glory.

The entire experience had a powerful and lasting impact on Fellowship Bible Church. The first Romanian hymnal cover to come off the printing press is now displayed in Plexiglas™ by the back door of the church auditorium for everyone to see. Nearby is a large world map that indicates where Fellowship-supported missionaries are located. The church's "Romanian Connection" is a constant reminder of the bonds of Christian unity—bonds that can best be forged when ministries are flexible and financially free.

WHY MINISTRIES FALL
INTO FINANCIAL BONDAGE

Christians do not set out to hinder or enslave their own ministries. Financial bondage just sort of "sneaks up" on them. Sadly, a ministry that ends up in dire financial straits usually inflicts its condition upon itself.

We've identified what we consider to be the six most common reasons that ministries find themselves in financial bondage:

- Ignorance
- Incomplete teaching
- Personal borrowing and debt
- Wrong motives
- Cultural conformance
- Limited giving

Ignorance

God's Word is replete with godly financial principles, but the church too often isn't teaching them. And in the absence of sound biblical teaching on debt and borrowing, ministries and families usually go about their business in the same way the world does. Ministries need to be teaching *and modeling* biblical financial principles, such as contentment, God's sovereignty, godly giving, borrowing cautions, debt warnings, saving, planning, and much more (for more details, refer to chapter 9).

The problem often starts in Bible colleges and seminaries, most of which do not teach about biblical financial principles. The result: Many of their graduates are ignorant of this vital area of biblical instruction. And when those graduates assume ministry roles, they are ill-equipped to teach on financial subjects. According to researchers John and Sylvia Ronsvalle, it's this very lack of training that makes pastors feel uncomfortable when teaching about money and financial matters.[7]

Incomplete Teaching

Despite the many Bible passages that teach financial principles, ministries too often provide incomplete instruction in the area of biblical finances. Churches are often adept at telling people what to do with the resources they give. But the Bible teaches people what to do with all their resources. That's why churches need to teach the *whole* counsel of God (Acts 20:27).

Because of the prevalence of incomplete teaching, too many ministries and congregations suffer financially. The lack of correct teaching on the subjects of borrowing and debt has resulted in far too many ministries—and Christian families—being in financial bondage.

Most of today's parachurch mission organizations have arisen because of the inadequate missions emphasis in many churches. In like manner, parachurch financial-teaching organizations such as Christian Financial Concepts, Crown Ministries, and others have arisen to "fill in" the financial teaching "gap" of many churches. But although parachurch financial-teaching organizations provide valuable resources, the *complete* message of God's financial principles *must* be taught from the pulpit. Then God's people will be fully "equipped for every good work" (2 Timothy 3:17).

Proper and complete financial teaching is important for all Christians, but especially so for those with greater financial challenges, such as single women, newlyweds, teens, and children. Children and teens need to learn good financial principles when they are young and moldable. Newlyweds need to get a handle on their finances before the loan-funded American culture overwhelms them and they wind up in debt or divorced. Single women (especially single moms) face their own set of unique challenges.

Comprehensive teaching on biblical finances also needs to be done systematically and carefully—an annual year-end giving sermon is not enough. To develop well-equipped stewards, financial teaching needs to be done *regularly,* according to a well-thought-out plan. Godly financial principles must also be presented in *proper biblical context,* as a vital part of a disciple's Christ-honoring lifestyle.

But financial concepts alone are not enough; there must be appropriate and practical *application* to enable people to incorporate the concepts into their lifestyles. Effective application might take the form of evening budgeting classes or a weekend seminar on wills and trusts that is taught by a committed Christian attorney.

Perhaps most important, financial principles and practices must be taught and *modeled* by ministry leadership. The "do as I say, not as I do" approach to financial teaching is a surefire way to short-circuit the kind of financial maturity that enables a ministry to grow without borrowing.

Personal Borrowing and Debt

Our experience in decades of financial counseling has shown us that the most common barrier that prevents American families from giving generously and sacrificially is the financial bondage that results from excessive borrowing and debt. But like blood that flows from a wound, borrowing and debt are not the real problems—they are but *symptoms* of the real problems. The financial "wounds" of American Christians are spiritual in nature, such as the inability to trust God's provision or a lack of contentment. And like a bleeding wound, the cut must be closed before the bleeding can be stopped and true healing can begin.

Those already burdened with payments are the ones who can least afford to take on more debt. When the average Christian's loan obligations begin to overwhelm him, one of the first budget items to get redirected toward loan repayment is giving to the local church. "How can you expect me to give when I owe so much?" is a lament we frequently hear in budget counseling. Generous giving has a difficult time competing with such credit-funded attractions as fine homes, expensive vacations, powerful new cars, flashy new electronics, and Christmas spending sprees.

In contrast, Jesus commanded his disciples in Matthew 6:19–21, "Do not store up for yourselves treasures on earth, where moth and rust destroy, and where thieves break in and steal. But store up for yourselves treasures in heaven, where moth and rust do not destroy, and where thieves do not break in and steal. For where your treasure is, there your heart will be also."

Easy credit makes it a simple matter to be financially extravagant, whether you're building a church or buying a new family car. Then, before you even realize it, your heart has wandered and you're in financial bondage—preoccupied with worldly things and entrapped by debt.

Wrong Motives

Some ministries, when faced with rapid growth or overwhelming financial challenges, borrow money simply in response to the perceived need. Although we generally disagree with the practice of ministry borrowing, we certainly cannot fault the genuine concern and care for God's work that motivates that kind of decision.

However, other ministries end up in financial bondage because they borrow money for the wrong motives. Some of those motives include greed, pride, and fear:

- *Greed.* Greed is the part of us that always wants more than we already have. Greed is never satisfied. Although most Americans don't take greed seriously, God does. According to Colossians 3:5, greed is idolatry—worshiping material things rather than the Creator of all things.

- *Pride.* In the course of our research we learned about a surprising number of pastors and ministry leaders who have driven churches into deep financial trouble by borrowing for no other reason than their own pride. Some pastors confessed that they secretly had wanted monuments to "their" accomplishments. Several were deeply sorry and wanted us to tell their stories so other ministries would not make their mistakes. As with greed, a no-borrowing, live-on-what-is-given policy can put an effective cap on the influence and outworkings of ministry pride.

- *Fear.* Some ministry leaders are actually competing against other growing ministries—they're afraid their ministries will shrink while others grow by taking "their" people. Other leaders feel that if they don't borrow to get the ideal building or property, they will somehow "miss out" on God's blessing. Still others are actually afraid to step out in financial faith, trusting God to supply every need through His people.

Ministry leaders need to take to heart what Paul said to Timothy, his young and fearful apprentice: "For God did not give us a spirit of timidity [KJV, fear], but a spirit of power, of love and of self-discipline" (2 Timothy 1:7).

People see only the outer appearance, but God knows the heart (1 Samuel 16:7). Prayerfully examine yourself and your ministry. Ask God to reveal any wrong motives, and then ask Him for the courage to deal with them.

Cultural Conformance

Borrowing is ingrained into the American culture. As a result, many Christians don't even question whether they should or shouldn't borrow. They just go ahead and do it without even *considering* other options.

For example, we spoke with a deacon from a growing church in upstate South Carolina. His church had just built a new multipurpose recreational and educational facility, financed with borrowed funds. The deacon told us, "I wasn't comfortable with borrowing all that money—but I didn't know there were any alternatives."

We've observed two kinds of cultural conformance that can victimize ministries. Some ministries simply fall in step with the world. But others blindly conform to "Christian" norms that are seldom challenged.

Worldly Conformance. The attitude of worldly financial experts is that "smart debt can be good for your finances."[8] However, Christians should note that *every* reference to borrowing in the Bible is either a warning or a caution.

We spoke with more than a few ministry leaders who presented elaborate reasoning to justify their loans, citing "good business reasons" for borrowing. Yet Christians must realize that ministry *cannot* be run as a secular business.

We're not suggesting that a ministry's business-related affairs should be conducted in anything less than a professional and businesslike manner. Rather, we believe that in ministry, biblical financial models *must* take precedence over those taught in American business schools. The biblical models for funding and expanding ministry are many, and they directly contradict those taught in most business schools.

"Christian" Conformance. Ministries often justify borrowing by citing other ministries that have borrowed and suffered no overtly negative consequences (such as division or bankruptcy). In fact, ministries that borrow and seem to be "successful" are often held up in the Christian community as models.

However, Christians must be careful not to evaluate the appropriateness of a practice solely on external results. After all, the end does not justify the means.

One of the biblical principles that ministries violate when they borrow is the "eternal investment" principle. Jesus clearly commanded Christians to invest in heavenly treasures, not earthly ones (Matthew 6:19–21). Paul described how the works of believers will someday be judged for their eternal value (1 Corinthians 3:12–15). Despite these admonitions, people often do not calculate the eternal impact that is lost when God's resources are rechanneled into interest payments to worldly lenders. For example:

- How many community action programs must be put on hold while a ministry is paying off loans at interest?

- How many missionaries can't be funded while a ministry is making loan and interest payments?

- How many believers are developing the attitude that they don't need to give generously because the church can just borrow what it needs?

- How many church members who cannot control their borrowing are being implicitly taught that borrowing is OK?

Yet ministries continue to pay off loans. Meanwhile, much vital ministry work goes undone. As Randy Alcorn has said, "Financial commitments and debts can be like spikes chained to our legs and driven into the ground, making us inflexible and unresponsive to God's call."[9]

There is perhaps no greater hindrance to the "good works" of ministry (1 Timothy 6:17–19) than the financial obligations that churches owe to their lenders.

Limited Giving

If people gave abundantly, few ministries would even consider borrowing. Why would they need to? Yet the problem of limited giving is not as simple as finding the switch in a dark room and flipping on the light—inadequate giving is the combined result of many ministry factors gone awry.

The bottom line is that too many of God's people fail to give liberally and sacrificially. Responding culturally and instinctively rather than scripturally, ministries feel pressured to borrow. Like the deacon in upstate South Carolina, many ministry leaders genuinely believe they have no other alternative.

Much of this book deals with the vital part that generous giving must play in the success of a non-borrowing ministry. That's because limited giving is one of the most serious problems facing American Christians, regardless of denomination. One of the finest biblical giving models is the Philippians, who, despite their extreme poverty, begged Paul for the privilege of giving (2 Corinthians 8:1–5). Yet how often does the modern American church emulate the Philippians' example?

America is the world's wealthiest nation. We are also the world's most selfish people, spending most of our vast resources on ourselves. According to Larry Burkett, "We do not suffer from a lack of money. We suffer from a lack of commitment to *give* the money."[10]

THE POTENTIAL CONSEQUENCES
OF LOAN-FUNDED MINISTRY

Borrowing is something like walking through a mine-field—you never know when the ground is going to explode

in your face. And like a mine explosion, the potential consequences of ministry borrowing can be disastrous. Some
of the consequences we've seen include:

- Disunity and resentment
- Ministry splits
- Reduced effectiveness
- Hampered growth
- Disbanding
- Legal action against ministry officers
- Poor testimony before the world

Disunity and Resentment

Borrowing has the power to create disharmony in a ministry like few other issues. We have observed that the concept of borrowing tends to polarize believers into two
mutually resentful camps. The anti-borrowing group claims
that those who want to borrow aren't trusting God; the pro-
borrowing group contends that those against borrowing are
fearful and overly conservative.

An example of the disunity that can result from borrowing is the situation of the small church described previously
in this chapter. The 250-member congregation had borrowed $750,000 through bonds, and 40 percent of the
church's income was going toward debt retirement. The associate pastor told of how various factions had arisen in the
church and were jockeying for positions of power. "All we
do anymore is fight over money," he lamented.

We're not implying that ministry borrowing always leads
to disunity. However, we believe that the risk is needlessly
high, especially in light of the fact that God has promised
to supply all the needs of His people (Philippians 4:19).

Ministry Splits

Continual and willful disobedience to biblical commands
to "live in harmony with one another" (Romans 12:16) has
tragic results. Disunity can evolve into something even
more undesirable: a split in the ministry. Factions can
become so polarized that they cannot resolve their differ-

ences. Each faction then goes its separate way, thus weakening a ministry's overall effectiveness and presenting a hypocritical testimony to the world.

We have observed far too many occasions of church splits that resulted from division over the issue of ministry borrowing. Perhaps one of the most notable is a very large church in Florida. After leading his church into a controversial, loan-financed, multimillion-dollar building program of awesome scope, the well-known senior pastor left the church. He took a significant number of members with him and began a new ministry, which soon began to draw additional members from his former church.

Thriving on the controversy, the press had a field day. As the pastor's former congregation dwindled to a fraction of its earlier size, the pressure of the ministry's financial obligations mounted further. A dynamic yet conservative new senior pastor was called, the church began to grow once again, and over several years it reduced its debt load to about four-fifths of its original total.

But after only a few years the conservative senior pastor resigned to take another position in another state. After he left, one of the church's long-time ministry leaders told us that many in the church were unhappy with what that pastor had done to reduce the church's debt. He also told us that the church's still-astronomical loan balance was making it difficult to attract a new senior pastor.

We're not suggesting that a church that borrows is doomed to split. But it happens more often than many of us realize. And pastors who have been through loan-induced financial crises are exhorting us to warn other ministries about the risk. So we caution you: "A prudent man sees danger and takes refuge, but the simple keep going and suffer for it" (Proverbs 22:3).

Reduced Effectiveness

If the church is the vehicle through which God reaches out to the world, borrowed funds can be like a tank of bad gasoline. Poor-quality fuel can slow you down or even bring you to a halt, leaving you stranded many miles from your destination.

Hampered Growth

Many claim that borrowing will stimulate ministry growth. Those who advocate borrowing claim that the excitement of a new ministry project will attract people. And the added giving from both existing and new members will help pay for the project.

However, thirty years of experience as a church architect and space-planner have taught Ray Bowman exactly the opposite. According to Bowman, "no church building, however perfectly designed, can make a church grow. The most a new building can do is allow a church to grow."[11] And borrowing only compounds the problem. As Bowman further states, "even conservative borrowing can put a church's ministries at unnecessary risk."[12] He cites one church that stagnated for twenty-nine years while repaying its mortgage![13]

Confirming our own experience, Bowman cites case after case in which the result of ministry borrowing was not growth, but stagnation or decline. The reason most often cited for failure to grow after borrowing is related to the financial pressure that ministries often bring to bear on their congregations and supporters to pay off the loan(s). A member of a loan-funded, 1,500-member midwestern church confessed, "I'd be embarrassed to invite any of my friends to our church, because they'd think the only reason I invited them was to get them to help pay the debt."[14]

Disbanding

It's tragic when ministries fail. It's especially tragic when they fail due to preventable causes, such as overborrowing and indebtedness.

When ministry leaders biblically commit to living within their means, they surrender control of the ministry's financial status into God's hands. Because God has promised to meet all the needs of selfless, sacrificial givers (Philippians 4:10–19), God's people can have confidence that their ministries will lack for nothing.

But when a ministry borrows, it begins living beyond its means, providing for itself that which a sovereign God has not. It's a recipe for disaster, as with the growing church of ministry profile 1.

Legal Action Against Ministry Officers

When a ministry fails, its creditors usually demand payment. Most ministry loans are issued by banks and other commercial lenders, rather than by fellow believers who are prepared to forgive the debt. In fact, creditors often go to great lengths to recover their money when a ministry fails. More than a few ministry leaders who personally guaranteed their ministry's loans have been pursued by the ministry's creditors.

Occasionally, aggressive creditors go much farther than just to the ministry's leaders in their efforts to recover their losses. In the case of one failed church, every family received a bill for many thousands of dollars from the ministry's chief creditor.

We're not saying that ministry borrowing ensures later bankruptcy and pursuit by creditors. But legal action is part of the serious risk that is closely linked to ministry borrowing.

Poor Testimony Before the World

From the earliest times in history, God has wanted His people to conform to the highest possible moral and ethical standards. He has always wanted His people to serve as a light to draw the world to Himself. Paul urged the Philippians, the people who sacrificed *in their poverty* to give to his missionary work, to "become blameless and pure, children of God without fault in a crooked and depraved generation, in which you shine like stars in the universe as you hold out the word of life" (Philippians 2:15–16).

In the financial arena, however, the modern American church does not shine. Rather than setting a high standard (faith), the church apes the world, operating at a low standard (borrowing). Experts say that America's biggest economic challenge is mushrooming debt (consumer, business, and governmental). Yet the church often does little to model or teach to the contrary.

A CHURCH IN BONDAGE

We've already explained that this was a difficult chapter to write. We conclude it with a final cautionary tale—one more pastor's tragic story of what happened when his church borrowed money. Note how many of the problems, disadvantages, and consequences we've presented in this chapter are present in this one ministry.

"Be Sure to Tell My Story"

One day Jim received a long-distance call from a fellow pastor. This man had met Jim at a CFC Pastor's Conference, one of many at which Jim has spoken in recent years. This pastor was calling Jim to apologize for not taking Jim's advice. He also wanted to encourage Jim to keep speaking about the benefits of ministering without borrowing. "And whenever you do," he said, beginning to weep, "be sure to tell my story and warn pastors that it could happen to them."

As with most church splits, nobody ever wanted it to happen—least of all the dedicated young pastor. But, as he tearfully reported, an ugly and embarrassing church split had left him defeated, discouraged, out of the ministry, and out of a job. Yet, even as he wept, he told of his firm resolve: If he ever again pastored a church, he would refuse to borrow money for ministry.

Borrowing: The Only Way?

He had been the pastor of a small but rapidly growing church in a medium-sized Texas city. Badly in need of more space, the church's leaders decided to refinance their mortgage and build a larger facility. The pastor admitted that he had wondered if borrowing was really God's best. But he went along with the plan; it seemed the only way to get the additional space the church needed.

However, within six months the area's economy collapsed. The church's growth slowed and then stopped. The costs of completing the new building exceeded the ministry's proposed budget, so the congregation was forced to go back to the bank and borrow more money at a higher interest rate. Giving began to decline, and people complained that all they ever heard about from the pulpit was money. Six families left the church when the deacons approved the mailing of tithe "reminder" cards to everyone on the church's mailing list—something that had never before been done.

With attendance and giving on a downward spiral, the loan payments became almost unbearable. All other sources of funding were eventually exhausted, and the church was forced to withdraw support from its missionaries. That prompted one of the ministry's most generous givers to leave the church in a storm of controversy.

How Much Are They Giving?

The pastor told Jim that every program in the church had suffered from crushing financial restrictions. New programs or activities were simply out of the question. But most tragic of all the church's problems was the pastor's growing materialistic focus. Sobbing, he confessed, "I started looking at people and wondering how much they were giving. I found myself calling first on visitors who lived in wealthy neighborhoods. Once I even neglected to reprimand an unruly child because he belonged to the wealthiest family in the church."

Finally, the ministry could no longer meet its loan payments. An emergency Wednesday-evening business meeting was called. Some wanted to declare bankruptcy, close the church, and reopen under another name. Some just wanted to close the church. Others proposed selling off assets, such as a portion of their modest property. The meeting was long, loud, and angry. In the end, thirty families walked out, vowing never to return.

Shortly thereafter, the young pastor resigned. During his call to Jim, he expressed doubts about ever returning to the ministry. The church, greatly reduced in size, had become the butt of the community's jokes and had nearly folded.

NOTES

1. Marvin Olasky, quoted in an article by John Zipperer, "Gambling Costs You More Than Money," *The Christian Reader,* July/August 1995 (accessed via America Online).

2. James Strong, *A Concise Dictionary of the Hebrew Bible* (1890; reprint New York: Abingdon Press, 1967), 59.

3. F. Delitzsch, *Proverbs, Ecclesiastes, and Song of Solomon,* trans. from German by James Martin, vol. 6 of *Commentary on the Old Testament,* by C. F. Keil and F. Delitzsch (1873; reprint Grand Rapids: Eerdmans, 1975), 87.

4. Philip Schaff, *Proverbs of Solomon,* vol. 5 of *Lange's Commentary on the Holy Scriptures,* ed. and trans. Philip Schaff (Grand Rapids: Zondervan, 1969), 192.

5. Ron Blue, *Master Your Money* (Nashville: Thomas Nelson, 1986), 63.

6. David Pollock, appearing on the "Money Matters" radio program, 12 June 1991.

7. "Members Get Richer But Not the Churches," *Orlando Sentinel,* 31 December 1994, D-5.

8. John Waggoner, "Low Rates Change the Rules," *USA Today,* 5 November 1993, 1B.

9. Randy Alcorn, *Money, Possessions, and Eternity* (Wheaton, Ill.: Tyndale, 1989), 197.

10. Larry Burkett, "Money Matters" radio program, 25 October 1991.

11. Ray Bowman with Eddy Hall, *When Not to Build* (Grand Rapids: Baker, 1992), 45.

12. Ibid., 88.

13. Ibid., 27–28.

14. Ibid., 29.

CHAPTER 4

A SURVEY OF SCRIPTURE
Examining the Biblical Pattern of Debt-Free Ministry

The Bible provides many examples of how God funds the work of the ministry. And as this survey of Scripture shows, *borrowing is contrary to the way God funded every ministry project in the Bible. God's plan has always been to meet ministry needs through the sacrificial giving of His people.* God always funds His ministry efforts—and He does it through His people.

Through carefully studying God's Word, we conclude that borrowing money is never God's best method for funding ministry needs. Throughout history, whether in Old or New Testament times, God has always provided ministry funds either before they were needed or as they were needed. And He has always done so through the generous, joyous, and sacrificial giving of His people—from resources He has already entrusted to them.

This chapter looks specifically at what the Bible says about ministry borrowing. It contains perhaps the most significant information in this entire book. In addition to an in-depth look at scriptural ministry models, we point out biblical cautions for those who are thinking of borrowing. The chapter concludes with a presentation of the most common Bible-based arguments used to defend ministry borrowing and provides a biblical response to each one.

BIBLICAL MODELS FOR MINISTRY FUNDING

God has been funding ministry for thousands of years. During that time, He has given us clear examples to follow. Excellent models of ministry funding can be found throughout the Bible, in both Old and New Testaments. We have selected six of those ministry models for this book, three each from the Old and New Testaments:

- Building the tabernacle
- Building the temple
- Restoring the temple
- Caring for those displaced at Pentecost
- Relieving famine in Jerusalem
- Supporting Paul's ministry

Let's examine each of these models in detail and look for common principles. We'll also pull in a few similar examples from ministries today.

Model 1: Building the Tabernacle
(Exodus 25:1–9, 35:20–29, and 36:4–7)

In contrast to the practices of the ancient world's pagan nations, God's people were to have only one place of worship—the temple. God first commanded the Hebrews to construct a portable temple, or tabernacle, for use during their time in the wilderness (Exodus 25–31).

While he was on Mount Sinai receiving the Law, Moses was given instructions to build a curtained courtyard one hundred fifty feet long by seventy-five feet wide. The tabernacle was to be made of forty-eight frameworks of acacia wood that were covered with gold. This portable structure was to be composed of two compartments—the "Holy Place" and the "Holy of Holies." Contained in these two compartments were to be an altar, a lampstand, a table, and an ornate golden box called the ark of the covenant.

Note two points concerning God's commands. First, His plans for the tabernacle were highly specific. Excruciatingly detailed in His instructions, God left little to the imagination. Second, the cost of the tabernacle has been estimated (in modern dollars) at more than $5 million.

Why are these points significant? The tabernacle was an extremely complex and expensive undertaking for a migrating nation. God was just as specific about *what to build* as He was in *how to fund it:*

> The Lord said to Moses, "Tell the Israelites to bring me an offering. You are to receive the offering for me from each man whose heart prompts him to give. These are the offerings you are to receive from them: gold, silver and bronze; blue, purple and scarlet yarn and fine linen; goat hair; ram skins dyed red and hides of sea cows; acacia wood; olive oil for the light; spices for the anointing oil and for the fragrant incense; and onyx stones and other gems to be mounted on the ephod and breastpiece. Then have them make a sanctuary for me, and I will dwell among them. Make this tabernacle and all its furnishings exactly like the pattern I will show you." (Exodus 25:1–9)

God was *specific* about the resources for the tabernacle and how they were to be collected. He instructed Moses "to receive the offering for me from each man whose heart prompts him to give" (v. 1). No compulsion, no coercion, not even a hint as to which families should give what. God's people were to fund God's project according to God's individual leading. And it worked! As we will see, this pattern for ministry funding is a consistent theme throughout God's Word.

Where to Find Resources? Where would the wandering children of Israel find the resources to build God's tabernacle? Mercifully, He had already supplied the necessary resources, courtesy of Egypt. Following the death of Egypt's firstborn males, the Pharaoh finally agreed to release the Hebrew people from slavery. Before leaving Egypt, God had one last task for His people to perform:

> The Israelites did as Moses instructed and asked the Egyptians for articles of silver and gold and for clothing. The Lord had made the Egyptians favorably disposed toward the people,

and they gave them what they asked for; so they plundered the Egyptians. (Exodus 12:35–36)

God plundered the Egyptians so His people would have what they needed in the wilderness to build the tabernacle. It is always God's plan to provide abundantly for His people so they, in turn, can experience the blessing of giving to His work (Acts 20:35). Paul clearly stated this principle to the church at Corinth:

He who supplies seed to the sower and bread for food will also supply and increase your store of seed and will enlarge the harvest of your righteousness. You will be made rich in every way so that you can be generous on every occasion, and through us your generosity will result in thanksgiving to God." (2 Corinthians 9:10–11)

The Challenge of Giving. The Bible does not say that giving is always easy or painless. Generous and sacrificial giving is *always* a difficult and challenging test of the will. In the case of Israel in the wilderness, it was no doubt very difficult for the former slaves to part with their recently acquired wealth. After all, there were no apparent means of income in the Sinai desert. Yet the people gave freely and generously—of their effort, their talents, and their possessions:

Everyone who was willing and whose heart moved him came and brought an offering to the Lord for the work on the Tent of Meeting, for all its service, and for the sacred garments. All who were willing, men and women alike, came and brought gold jewelry of all kinds: brooches, earrings, rings and ornaments. They all presented their gold as a wave offering to the Lord. Everyone who had blue, purple or scarlet yarn or fine linen, or goat hair, ram skins dyed red, or hides of sea cows brought them. Those presenting an offering of silver or bronze brought it as an offering to the Lord, and everyone who had acacia wood for any part of the work brought it. (Exodus 35:21–24)

The people's response was overwhelming—so much so that Moses finally had to put a stop to it when they re-

ceived more than was actually needed (Exodus 36:4–7). When was the last time something like this happened in your church?

The biblical pattern is clear, even in 1400 B.C.: God blesses His people with resources. A ministry need arises. God impresses His people to give generously, joyously, and sacrificially. The need is met. And God gets the praise.

Model 2: Building the Temple
(1 Chronicles 29:1–20)

In 1000 B.C., King David was moved by God to build a permanent place of worship in the city of Jerusalem. It was to be a "palace of cedar" and, with God's blessing, would "continue forever" (2 Samuel 7:1–27). Yet David was told by God that because he was a man of war, he would not be permitted to build it. His son Solomon, the next king, would actually build the temple (1 Chronicles 22:6–10).

Solomon would build, but David's part was to accumulate. He was to gather the resources needed for building a temple of "great magnificence and fame and splendor in the sight of all the nations" (1 Chronicles 22:5). Such a massive and expensive project would require extraordinary funding (some have estimated the cost of the temple at more than *$3 billion*). How did God, through David, command the money and materials to be gathered? David told the whole assembly:

> In my devotion to the temple of my God I now give my personal treasures of gold and silver for the temple of my God, over and above everything I have provided for this holy temple: three thousand talents of gold (gold of Ophir) and seven thousand talents of refined silver, for the overlaying of the walls of the buildings, for the gold work and the silver work, and for all the work to be done by the craftsmen. (1 Chronicles 29:3–5)

After promising great stores of his own wealth, the king asked, "Now, *who is willing to consecrate himself today to the Lord?*" (v. 5b, italics added). Scripture records the response of Israel's leaders: "Then the *leaders of families*, the *officers of the tribes* of Israel, the *commanders* of thousands and *commanders* of hundreds, and the *officials* in charge of the king's work gave willingly" (v. 6, italics added). After that, "The people rejoiced at the *willing response of their leaders,* for they had given freely and wholeheartedly to the Lord. David the king also rejoiced greatly" (v. 9, italics added).

What an awesome example of funding God's work in God's way! Following David's example, the Israelite leaders were inspired to give "freely and wholeheartedly."

So what does "wholeheartedly" really *mean,* in modern terms? Estimating a talent to be seventy-five pounds, David gave out of his personal fortune *110 tons of gold* and *260 tons of silver.* This was apparently in addition to the vast amount of giving he had already done when he personally commissioned Solomon to build (1 Chronicles 22:14).

When all was said and done, the total amount of gold, silver, and bronze David and the leaders gave (22:14; 29:4, 7) totaled a massive *46,610 tons,* or *93.22 million pounds*— not counting the other materials gathered. (We wonder: How dramatically would churches see their congregational giving increase if their own leaders set the example?)

What should we make of this incredible outpouring of generosity? Did David and his leaders take pride in their accomplishment? Hardly. We encourage you to meditate on David's prayer:

> But who am I, and who are my people, that we should be able to give as generously as this? Everything comes from you, and we have given you only what comes from your hand. We are aliens and strangers in your sight, as were all our forefathers. Our days on earth are like a shadow, without hope. O Lord our God, as for all this abundance that we have provided for building you a temple for your Holy Name, it comes from your hand, and all of it belongs to you. (1 Chronicles 29:14–20)

Note the interrelationship—the *interdependence*—between generous giving and spiritual commitment: When David shared his testimony of personal giving and then asked his captains, "Now, who is willing to consecrate himself today to the Lord?" (29:5), they knew what he was talking about. They understood that their giving was an outward indicator of their inner devotion to God.

David later prayed that the desire to give willingly would remain in the hearts of the people *and* that God would keep their hearts loyal to Him (29:17–18). Paul had the same concern for the Corinthian church (2 Corinthians 8:7–8). Both Paul and David understood that giving is a direct reflection of one's commitment to and love for God.

Our prayer is that God would help today's American church to think, and worship, and give in this way!

Model 3: Restoring the Temple
(2 Kings 12:1–12; 2 Chronicles 24:8–14)

Joash was king of Judah for forty years (from 835 to 796 B.C.). For many of those years he was a godly king who, according to 2 Kings 12:2, "did what was right in the eyes of the Lord." One of the right things Joash did was to restore Solomon's temple.

The temple, through a succession of wicked kings, had fallen into disrepair. Joash's fund-raising method was unique in the Old Testament. It's another example of how God provides for His work through the giving of His people:

> At the king's command, a chest was made and placed outside, at the gate of the temple of the Lord. A proclamation was then issued in Judah and Jerusalem that they should bring to the Lord the tax that Moses the servant of God had required of Israel in the desert. All *the officials and all the people brought their contributions gladly,* dropping them into the chest until it was full. Whenever the chest was brought in by the Levites to the king's officials and they saw that there was a large amount of money, the royal secretary and the officer of the chief priest would come and empty the chest and carry it back to its place. (2 Chronicles 24:8–11, italics added)

Tomorrow's Ministry with Today's Money. Note that Joash did not commission the work and then try to figure out how to pay for it. He collected the money *first,* and *then* he had the work done. The context also indicates that after the restoration had begun, some work was paid for as it was being done. The most common modern method is to pay for today's ministry with tomorrow's money. Joash was careful to pay for *tomorrow's* ministry with *today's* money.

It's also important to see how the people responded to Joash's plan. In the years leading up to the restoration of the temple, the nation's giving had become so anemic that the amount was barely enough to care for the priests and Levites. No money was available for work on the temple (2 Kings 12:4–6). Yet when Joash began his "campaign chest," an abundance of money was soon available. So great were the offerings that the chest had to be repeatedly emptied until, at last, they had "met all the other expenses of restoring the temple" (2 Kings 12:12).

The fund-raising methods of Joash illustrate a key giving principle: God's people are often more impressed to give when they see a direct link between their gifts and God's working. In modern terms, the application of this principle might be described as "Give and we will build." Or, stated in the negative, "Don't give—and we won't build."

To fund God's work with a bank loan robs people of a clear, godly motive for giving. God has already entrusted to His people the resources they need to accomplish any ministry He desires. Freeing up those resources is simply a matter of believers sacrificially following God's giving principles by faith and then trusting Him to provide. Do you want to transform apathetic giving into enthusiastic giving? Try the "Joash Principle."

Applying God's Lessons in America. In the early 1980s, Jim Burgess and his congregation at Fellowship Bible Church had the firsthand opportunity to learn about the blessings of generous, freewill giving. In the fall of 1982, the elders established becoming debt-free as one of their primary ministry goals for 1983. At that time the church owed a little over $100,000 on its building. The elders had calculated that accelerated mortgage payments would enable the church to completely pay off its loan by December 1983.

The accelerated mortgage payments began, and Fellowship was on its way to being loan-free. Then God started working in a big way. In March 1983, a house next door to the church went up for sale. The asking price: $74,000. Due to its growth, Fellowship desperately needed that house. People were already meeting in five homes for Sunday school and visitors were leaving when they couldn't find a place to park.

The house was exactly what the growing church needed. In fact, the church board was tempted to break their non-borrowing commitment, get a loan, and buy the house. They were even more tempted when a wealthy new member came to them and said he would donate $20,000 as a down payment if the church would borrow the rest and buy the house. After a week of prayer and fasting, the board unanimously voted not to borrow. They were committed to trusting God to supply all their financial needs— in a way that only *He* could.

The board went back to the new member with a different proposal: They would ask the woman who owned the house to give the church sixty days to raise the money in cash. Any funds raised to buy the house would be *in addition to* the church's accelerated mortgage payments. If the money could be raised, they would purchase the house. But if the money didn't come in, the board would conclude that God had other plans.

The new member laughed, shook his head, and then said, "I've never heard of doing business that way and I don't think it'll work. But, if that's what you want to do, go ahead." The board had hoped the new member would offer his $20,000 to start the fund. He did not. The owner of the house asked for $1,000 in nonrefundable earnest money. Fellowship's elders, not wanting to put church funds at risk, raised the $1,000 among themselves.

The Evidence of Things Hoped for. For the first few weeks the money came in very slowly. The elders grew concerned, and they began to fast and pray. Jim knew how much the congregation needed the house and how important the issue had become to the church. He was tempted to secretly borrow the money himself. The board members began to ask: Will God truly supply the funds for "every good work" (2 Corinthians 9:8)?

Gradually, the elders began to see more and more contributions earmarked for "The House." But no large amounts. In fact, no gift was over a few thousand dollars. Yet every person in the congregation seemed to understand the urgency of the situation. Many people gave again and again as God urged them. One Sunday the church received a deed to a ski boat. On another Sunday, a widow's wedding ring. The Wednesday-night prayer meeting grew as people gathered to pray for "The House."

On May 30, 1983, the sixty-day fund-raising period came to an end. At that point the congregation didn't have $74,000 in cash—they had *$88,000!* God, working through the sacrificial generosity of His people, had provided more than enough to purchase the house and remodel it for ministry use. In addition, Fellowship never missed an accelerated mortgage payment. The church paid off its loan in December 1983, right on schedule.

Model 4: Caring for Those Displaced at Pentecost
(Acts 2:44–45; 4:32–35)

We've seen from the Old Testament that when God directed ministry, He provided the funding either before the ministry effort began or as it was being accomplished. And we've seen that God never used loans. Rather, He met ministry needs through the generous, joyous, and sacrificial giving of His own people.

It's important to note that God's fund-raising methods apply to more than just building projects in ancient Israel. God used the same principles to build lives in the New Testament. A classic example of God's New Testament ministry-provision principles is the way the infant church cared for those with material needs.

As a result of the outpouring of God's Spirit at Pentecost, thousands of people came to Christ immediately (Acts 2:41, 47). The conversions continued in huge numbers in the days, weeks, and months that followed. Many of the newly saved were Jewish pilgrims who had come from all over the Roman world to Jerusalem for the Feast of Pentecost. Thousands of those new believers in "The Way" (Acts 9:2) remained in Jerusalem after the feast to learn from the apostles and grow in their newfound faith.

Overwhelming Benevolence Needs. Almost immediately the early church was faced with an overwhelming challenge. How were the new converts to be housed, fed, clothed, and cared for? Should they send the new Christians back home to their churchless cities? Should they admit the obvious, that no funds were available to meet the new believers' needs? How could they handle the problem? As always, God provided a way:

> All the believers were one in heart and mind. No one claimed that any of his possessions was his own, but they shared everything they had. . . . There were no needy persons among them. For from time to time those who owned lands or houses sold them, brought the money from the sales and put it at the apostles' feet, and it was distributed to anyone as he had need. (Acts 4:32, 34, 35)

This compassionate sharing of food and possessions enabled the early church to care for its own during a time of great economic crisis. John MacArthur explains that the new believers were honoring a "long-standing tradition in Israel during the great religious feasts." Ordinary people opened their homes for those people whom the inns could not hold. But, says John MacArthur, this "was not a primitive form of communism."

> They did not at any point sell everything and pool the proceeds into a common pot. Such a principle for Christian living would have obviated the responsibility of each believer to give in response to the Spirit's prompting (cf. 1 Corinthians 16:1–2). Further, it is clear from verse 46 that individuals still owned homes. What actually happened was that personal property was sold *as anyone might have need*. It was an indication of immense generosity, as people gave not only their present cash or goods, but also their future in acts of sacrificial love to those in need.[1]

Again the biblical pattern is clear: God directs His people to give so His work can be accomplished. He is always

faithful to provide those who love Him with whatever resources they need for any good work. All God requires of
His people is that they be open conduits through which His
resources can flow freely. Borrowing and debt always hinder—and sometimes even stop—the flow of God's resources
by diverting them to non-ministry priorities, such as luxury
purchases, interest payments, or even bond retirement.

Hurricane Results in Ministry Opportunity. Consider,
for example, how God worked in a south Florida Presbyterian church. Immanuel Presbyterian Church of Kendall
experienced a benevolence crisis similar to that of the early church. Had the people not been following biblical financial principles, they would have missed out on a truly
inspiring opportunity for ministry and the subsequent
blessings that flowed from their response.

In 1990, Pastor Al Lacour and his fellow church leaders
decided not to borrow money to expand and remodel their
overtaxed facility. Instead they chose to trust God's people
to give. They made the decision not to build until most of
the needed funds were raised in cash and the remainder
was covered by "faith pledges." By August 1992, with more
than three-fourths of the money in the bank, they decided
to start building.

Two days before the scheduled groundbreaking, Hurricane Andrew (one of the most devastating storms in recorded history) struck south Florida. Kendall, located in
southwest Dade County, was hard hit. Many members of
Immanuel Presbyterian suffered significant losses.

Quickly, Pastor Lacour and the church elders voted to
use the building fund for hurricane relief. By God's grace,
the church facility had suffered minimal damage in com-
parison to other churches. Even so, the elders reasoned,
how could they expand and improve the church buildings
when many of their own members were homeless? During
the next few weeks the church gave away more than
$300,000 to its members for food, clothing, housing, auto-
mobiles, medical costs, and so forth. The ministry committed to meet the needs of hurting people in a New
Testament way.

As a result of the church's sacrificial giving, God has been faithful to Immanuel Presbyterian (Philippians 4:14–19). The church has since grown significantly, especially in the number of young families. The community saw what the church was doing, and people care much more about what Christians *do* than what they *say they believe*.

Pastor Lacour, now ministering in Atlanta, says that Hurricane Andrew was a God-given ministry opportunity that came as a blessing in disguise for Immanuel Presbyterian. After the hurricane, the church once again raised the money to build, and it has since finished its new construction. The congregation has grown in number and in spirit, largely due to their willingness to trust God and follow His biblical pattern for funding ministry.

Model 5: Relieving Famine in Jerusalem
(1 Corinthians 16:1–3; 2 Corinthians 8:1–15)

By about A.D. 55, the Christians in Jerusalem were again in need. As prophesied in Acts 11:28 and recorded by Josephus,[2] a severe famine struck the entire Roman world during the reign of the emperor Claudius (A.D. 41–54). Jerusalem and its environs were especially needy. The city itself, being regularly overpopulated with pilgrims and other visitors, suffered the most.

The Christians of Jerusalem had been intensely persecuted for their faith and had lost much of their economic strength. They were left almost destitute as a result of the famine. How did the Christians of other areas respond? According to Acts 11, "The disciples, each according to his ability, decided to provide help for the brothers living in Judea. This they did, sending their gift to the elders by Barnabas and Saul" (vv. 29–30).

As at Pentecost when the church was born, this was genuine ministry need. The believers in Jerusalem were in desperate trouble. And as He had done throughout history, God met their need through the generous giving of His people. Paul and Barnabas were assigned the task of collecting the relief funds from the various churches throughout the

Roman world. While in Ephesus, Paul wrote the church in Corinth to instruct them regarding their participation:

> Now about the collection for God's people: Do what I told the Galatian churches to do. On the first day of every week, each one of you should set aside a sum of money in keeping with his income, saving it up, so that when I come no collections will have to be made. Then, when I arrive, I will give letters of introduction to the men you approve and send them with your gift to Jerusalem. (1 Corinthians 16:1–3)

The Macedonian Model for Giving. Later, in his second letter, Paul encouraged and challenged the Corinthian believers to give by telling of the great generosity of the Macedonian churches:

> And now, brothers, we want you to know about the grace that God has given the Macedonian churches. Out of the most severe trial, their overflowing joy and their extreme poverty welled up in rich generosity. For I testify that they gave as much as they were able, and even beyond their ability. Entirely on their own, they urgently pleaded with us for the privilege of sharing in this service to the saints. And they did not do as we expected, but they gave themselves first to the Lord and then to us in keeping with God's will. (2 Corinthians 8:1–5)

When Paul described the Macedonian churches (Philippi, Thessalonica, and Berea) as experiencing "severe trial" and "extreme poverty," he was not exaggerating. All the Christians in Macedonia had suffered persecution and economic hardship. When writing to the Thessalonian church, Paul referred to the "severe suffering" (1 Thessalonians 1:6) they had endured. He compared their persecutions to those suffered by the Jerusalem church at the hands of the Jews (2:14). As described repeatedly in the book of Acts, such persecution often included beatings, stonings, banishment, criminal charges, imprisonment, and even death. No doubt many of the Thessalonians' own "countrymen" had stopped doing business with the believers, thus making their economic plight all the more severe.

Paul knew firsthand how difficult the conditions were for the Macedonian Christians. On his second missionary journey (Acts 16), he was beaten in Philippi, forced to sneak out of Thessalonica by night, and chased out of Berea by unruly mobs. Macedonia was not an easy place to be a Christian, nor for a Christian to make a living.

Poor People, Rich Generosity. Yet Paul said in 2 Corinthians 8 that the Macedonians gave with "rich generosity." They did not give out of any sort of abundance—they gave out of their *extreme poverty*. And as commentator Murray Harris says, "Their poverty no more impeded their generosity than their tribulation diminished their joy."[3]

In contrast, today's American church knows little of this kind of giving. Rarely do American Christians give when it hurts or until it hurts. Normal American practice is to give out of what's left over after spending lavishly on ourselves and our families. Research has shown time and again that the average American Christian almost never gives any amount that would necessitate a reduced standard of living.

Is that truly biblical giving? Is that the New Testament way? God's plan for accomplishing His work is that His people should give willingly, generously, joyously, and *sacrificially*. And because God's plan is so unlike the world's methods, *only God* can get the glory when His plan works.

Model 6: Supporting Paul's Ministry
(Philippians 4:10–20)

One of the most common arguments used to support ministry borrowing is the importance of winning people to Christ. By this way of thinking, it is more important to evangelize than to debate the fine biblical points about borrowing money. Some ministries have even used the soul-winning argument to justify major indebtedness. Is this biblical? Is this God's plan? Not according to the example of how the apostle Paul's ministry was funded.

Winning the lost was what drove Paul to the ends of the earth (1 Corinthians 9:19–23), and that goal must remain at the very heartbeat of the church. But there is no record of Paul ever borrowing money. Nor did Paul ever advise a church to borrow money for ministry. His entire support came either from his own tentmaking work (Acts 18:1–4; 20:34–35; and 1 Corinthians 4:12) or from the faithful giving of other believers—especially the church at Philippi.

According to 2 Corinthians 11:7–9, the sacrificial gifts of the Philippian church made possible Paul's lengthy stay at Corinth. He was able to minister for eighteen months in Corinth from about A.D. 51–52. About ten years later Paul wrote the Philippians to thank them, not only for his early ministry support, but for other gifts he had also received from them:

> It was good of you to share in my troubles. Moreover, as you Philippians know, in the early days of your acquaintance with the gospel . . . not one church shared with me in the matter of giving and receiving, except you only . . . [but] you sent me aid again and again when I was in need. Not that I am looking for a gift, but I am looking for what may be credited to your account. I have received full payment and even more; I am amply supplied, now that I have received from Epaphroditus the gifts you sent. They are a fragrant offering, an acceptable sacrifice, pleasing to God. And my God will meet all your needs according to his glorious riches in Christ Jesus. To our God and Father be glory for ever and ever. Amen. (Philippians 4:14–20)

Notice three vital points that Paul stressed to the Philippians:

- *God found their gifts pleasing* (v. 18). God is pleased when we give to support the work of the ministry. Paul called it a "fragrant offering, an acceptable sacrifice." He used the Old Testament analogy of burning aromatic incense on an altar as a symbol of worship. In many cases, the Bible describes acceptable offerings as a "pleasing aroma to the Lord." (Such passages include Genesis 8:20–21; Exodus 29:18; and Leviticus 1:9, 13, 17.) Most significantly, Paul used this same phrase, "fragrant offering," to describe Christ's gift of Himself for us on the cross (Ephesians 5:2). Paul considered the sacrificial support of the Philippians to be worthy of his highest praise.

- *God promised to meet their needs as a* result *of their generous giving* (v. 19). This verse is often quoted, but frequently misunderstood. It is a promise from God that those who give will be given to (Luke 6:38). Paul was saying, "You Philippians supplied my needs; now God will supply your needs. I have received full payment and so shall you." This is not a "prosperity gospel" heresy, nor is it a "give to get" mentality. We may not receive rewards at all—until we reach heaven. The real "glory" of Christ's riches are not in this world. But clearly Paul was telling believers that God is aware of the faithfulness of their giving, and He will make sure they are fully compensated.

- *God would get all the glory for their giving* (v. 20). When God provides supernaturally as only He can, He gets all the glory. Yet far too often, new buildings or ministry growth bring glory to the people who made it happen—or to the bank that provided the loan. Building committees and successful fund-raisers have become heroes in the modern church. We seem to be able to accomplish incredible things—as long as the economy stays on track and our credit holds out. It sometimes seems it's not as important what the Lord desires as what the loan officer allows. Is God getting all the glory for our ministry accomplishments? Or is part of the credit going to First National Bank?

Paul points out that as a result of the Philippians' gifts, God and God alone will be glorified. Only God can impress people to give generously in spite of "extreme poverty." Only God can get the glory when His work is funded through the joyous, sacrificial giving of His people.

As we can see from God's Word, God has a definite and successful plan for funding ministry. Whether in the Old or New Testaments, *sacrificial giving is the pattern for funding every type of ministry project in the Bible.* Dare we use any other methods to fund God's work than those endorsed time and again by God Himself?

BIBLICAL CAUTIONS AGAINST BORROWING

In addition to ignoring the many scriptural examples of "borrow-free" ministry, we ignore important biblical cautions when we borrow to fund God's work. As with any of God's principles, He gives us the freedom to follow His advice or to go our own way. We can use His Word as our guide or suffer the consequences.

For the purposes of this book, we have identified five biblical cautions against borrowing money to fund ministry:

- Borrowing is enslavement.
- Borrowing weakens the testimony of God's provision.
- Borrowing often presumes on the future.
- Borrowing often indicates a lack of trust in God.
- Borrowing often reflects discontentment with God's provision.

Caution 1: Borrowing Is Enslavement

For Israel, God equated borrowing with enslavement, servitude, and subservience. The Mosaic Law presented borrowing as a practice that God's people could avoid if they remained faithful to Him:

> The Lord will open the heavens, the storehouse of his bounty, to send rain on your land in season and to bless all the work of your hands. You will lend to many nations but will borrow from none. The Lord will make you the head, not the tail. If you pay attention to the commands of the Lord your God that I give you this day and carefully follow them, you will always be at the top, never at the bottom. (Deuteronomy 28:12–13)

God intended Israel to be a nation of lenders, not borrowers. The parallelism of the Hebrew language structure used in Deuteronomy 15:6 equates "lending" with "ruling" and "borrowing" with being "ruled over." The word translated "rule" ("reign" in the King James Version) is *mashal*. It means "to govern or have dominion over."[4] The word is frequently used in the Old Testament to describe God's rightful rule of the earth and all it contains (2 Chronicles 20:6; Psalms 89:9; 103:19). King David used the word in his prayer of praise at the gathering of resources for the building of the temple: "Wealth and honor come from you; you are the ruler of all things" (1 Chronicles 29:12).

"No man can serve two masters." God wants to be our *exclusive* ruler. Borrowing always leads to people and things ruling over us. As a result, we too often find ourselves, as Deuteronomy 28:13 says, being the "tail" instead of the "head," or on the "bottom" instead of the "top." Ministries that borrow money are *always* servants to their lenders. God clearly warns of this in Proverbs 22 where the word *mashal* is again used: "The rich rule over the poor, and the borrower *is* servant to the lender" (Proverbs 22:7, emphasis added). Your servitude may be easy or hard; your lender may be a kind taskmaster or a harsh one. But when you borrow, you *do* become the lender's slave.

In contrast, God wants to pour out His riches on His people, preventing them from ever having to borrow. If we simply live by His principles, He will supply everything we need from the "storehouse of His bounty." As non-borrowing ministries across America eagerly testify, God is able to give much more than anyone could ever borrow from any worldly source.

Caution 2: Borrowing Weakens the Testimony of God's Provision

The means by which God funds His work is evidence of His blessing and love. When we step aside from His best plan, we reduce the impact of His working in and through us. Consider what God said to Israel:

> If you fully obey the Lord your God and carefully follow all his commands I give you today, the Lord your God will set you high above all the nations on earth. . . . The Lord will establish you as his holy people, as he promised you on oath, if you keep the commands of the Lord your God and walk in his ways. *Then all the peoples on earth will see that you are called by the name of the Lord,* and they will fear you. The

Lord will grant you abundant prosperity—in the fruit of your womb, the young of your livestock and the crops of your ground—in the land he swore to your forefathers to give you. (Deuteronomy 28:1, 9–11, italics added)

God wanted to make the Israelites a model for all the world. His desire was to set her "high above all the nations of the earth." If Israel was obedient, they would be granted such "abundant prosperity" that every aspect of their lives would be supernaturally blessed. Why did God want this? The answer is in verse 10: "Then all the peoples on earth will see that you are called by the name of the Lord, and they will fear you."

The word "fear" in Hebrew is *yare* and means in this context, "awe, astonishment, or wonderment."[5] God's plan for Israel was that all other nations would look at His supernatural provision for Israel and be forced to acknowledge His eternal existence. Through Israel, the other peoples of the earth would come to faith in the one true God.

God's supernatural provision for His people is one of the most powerful aspects of our testimony to an unbelieving world. When we step aside from His direct provision, we lessen the impact of our testimony. What's supernatural about Christians if we fund God's work with the world's methods? If we build churches the same way we build shopping malls and bowling alleys, how can God be glorified?

Pastor Kim Alexander of non-borrowing Spirit Lake Baptist Church commented on his church's recent completion of its 250-seat auditorium: "We serve the same God as Abraham, Moses, and Joshua. God was faithful to all of them. That same God can and will provide for us today. Now if you say, 'We've got to build tomorrow,' then you'll probably have to borrow. But if you expand your ministry on God's timetable, you won't need to borrow."[6]

Larry Burkett summarized this principle well when he said, "To minister without borrowing becomes a testimony to God and not a testimony to man's ingenuity. We are an ingenious people and can accomplish much without God's involvement. . . . Borrowing keeps us from seeing God work

supernaturally in many of our churches. God wants to perform miracles, we instead substitute mortgages."[7]

Caution 3: Borrowing Often Presumes on the Future

The Bible warns us not to presume on the future. We
must not assume anything that seems easy today can be
easily done tomorrow. The book of James offers a powerful
warning about presumption:

> Now listen, you who say, "Today or tomorrow we will go to
> this or that city, spend a year there, carry on business and
> make money." Why, you do not even know what will happen
> tomorrow. What is your life? You are a mist that appears for a
> little while and then vanishes. Instead, you ought to say, "If it
> is the Lord's will, we will live and do this or that." As it is, you
> boast and brag. All such boasting is evil. (James 4:13–16)

James tells us that presuming on tomorrow is *sin*. James
calls it "evil" and uses the Greek word *poneros* which "de-
notes evil that causes pain, sorrow, or suffering."[8] Presuming on tomorrow ultimately brings heartache and pain to
all involved. It's a foolish and harmful thing to do. We have
no promise of tomorrow. Our lives are fragile and can be
changed—or even extinguished—in an instant.

Borrowing money, especially for extended periods (e.g.,
more than seven years), is presuming on the future. When
we borrow, we naively make several potentially dangerous
(if not outright false) assumptions:

- Our future will be just as or more financially secure
  than today.
- Even though God has not funded a project, it is still
  His will to do it now.
- Our ministry will be in operation long enough to
  pay back the loan.

None of these assumptions is either guaranteed or wise.
Our fragile economy could experience an economic "earth-
quake" at any time. A natural disaster or the premature

death of a pastor or prominent ministry leader could completely change our plans.

Caution 4: Borrowing Often Indicates a Lack of Trust in God

Borrowing is not a brave and trusting act of faith in the
sovereign Provider, but a retreat into the comfortable
world of sight and self-provision. We are commanded in
Scripture to trust God for His provision, not to supplement
His goodness with our own financial plans. Biblical trust is
faith in God plus nothing, not faith in God plus our good
credit rating or faith in God plus favorable mortgage terms.

Trusting God completely to fund a ministry project is
not walking by "sight," as some falsely claim. Walking by
sight is seeing borrowed money in the bank before beginning construction, and then presuming that it can somehow be paid back. Walking by "faith" is beginning with a
zero bank balance and admitting to God that nothing will
ever happen unless He provides.

Caution 5: Borrowing Often Reflects
Discontentment with God's Provision

Borrowing almost always reflects a lack of contentment.
It's been said that if we're not content where we are, we'll
never be happy when we get where we're going. In contrast, Paul was content even when he had to "do without"
what he considered to be necessary (Philippians 4:11–12).
Can we say the same of ourselves?

We borrow because we're not content with God's present provision. It's as if we're saying, "We don't have what
we need. God hasn't provided us with enough funds to accomplish His ministry. So let's get the funding from some-
where else. Then we can get what we want without waiting
for it." Such thinking is contrary to the clear teaching of
Scripture.

In Philippians 4:11–13, Paul explains the oft-quoted (but
often misunderstood) principle of contentment. He then
praises God for meeting his needs—not with a loan, but by
means of the Philippians' sacrificial generosity. In Hebrews
13:5, Christians are clearly *commanded* to be content:
The writer says, "Keep your lives free from the love of

money and be content with what you have, because God
has said, 'Never will I leave you; never will I forsake you.'"

The Greek word translated "content" in both these passages is *autarkes*. This word comes from Stoic philosophy
and includes the idea of self-sufficiency, or being able to
get along without help. Describing this word, John Walvoord
writes, "It is not contentment arising from an abundance of
things, but an inner adjustment to outer circumstances. In
Paul's case, this resulted from spiritual grace."[9]

By God's grace, Paul was able to get by, to make do, to
accept any situation whether he was living in plenty or in
want. Today, most Christians know how to be happy only
in times of plenty. If they don't have what they want or
what they think they need, they find some way of getting
it, often borrowing money to do so.

People are quick to quote Philippians 4:13, where Paul
said, "I can do everything through him who gives me
strength." But do they really mean it? Are Christians willing to wait for God and refuse to rush ahead of His sovereign plan for funding ministry? Are God's people willing to
make do with what they have and creatively use it until
God supplies something else?

ARGUMENTS TO THE CONTRARY

Some disagree with the conclusions of this chapter.
They say that the Bible doesn't discourage borrowing, and
that our interpretations of Scripture are incorrect. Some
claim that the Bible actually supports or even encourages
borrowing. What arguments do they use? And what ought
to be our scriptural response?

Often people will object to non-borrowing ministry on
what they mistakenly consider to be biblical grounds.
We've identified seven of these "biblical" arguments that
people often put forward to justify or defend ministry
borrowing:

- The Bible actually says very little about borrowing
  or debt.

- Most verses about borrowing are in the Old Testament and are not relevant today.
- Because it commends lending, the Bible actually supports the concept of borrowing.
- The Bible recommends borrowing, because Elisha told a widow to borrow jars.
- Forbidding people to borrow is legalistic.
- We can win the lost by borrowing, so it must be within God's will.
- Borrowing is an act of faith.

Argument 1: The Bible actually says very little about borrowing or debt.

Response: It's not important whether Scripture says a little or a lot. The real issue is *what* Scripture says.

A search of the Bible reveals that the words "loan," "lend," "borrow," "credit," "debt," or "repay" occur (in a monetary sense) in the NIV a total of thirty-eight times in the Old Testament and ten times in the New Testament. So, comparatively speaking, it's true the Bible does not make frequent references to borrowing. But does that mean we should ignore what it says or consider the subject unimportant? Consider how often the following subjects are mentioned in the NIV:

- *Steal, steals, stealing*—eighteen times in the Old Testament; thirteen times in the New Testament
- *Envy, envying, envious*—twelve times in the Old Testament; seventeen times in the New Testament
- *Greed, greedy, greediness*—ten times in the Old Testament; fifteen times in the New Testament

Like borrowing and debt, the topics of stealing, envy, and greed are all mentioned only a few times in the Bible. Should we therefore conclude that they are not important subjects to God? Remember that some of these citations are in the Ten Commandments! The answer, of course, is that it doesn't matter how often the Bible speaks about a subject. It's what the Bible actually *says* that's important.

Remember that God does not say borrowing is sin—He says it's *risky*. He warns against it. And what God cautions His people about is vitally important and should be the concern of every Christian.

Argument 2: Most verses about borrowing are in the Old Testament and are not relevant today.

Response: It's true that most Scripture passages that relate to borrowing are in the Old Testament. However, examples in the Old Testament *are* relevant to modern American Christians.

Paul clearly states in 2 Timothy 3:16 that "All Scripture is God-breathed and is useful for teaching, rebuking, correcting and training in righteousness." What we sometimes forget is that he was referring *primarily to the Old Testament* at the time of his writing.

Argument 3: Because it commends lending, the Bible actually supports the concept of borrowing.

Response: Believers are commanded to be lenders, but they are actively cautioned against borrowing. The fact that God endorses lending does not mean He favors borrowing.

Those who advocate borrowing point out that the Mosaic Law has guidelines and admonitions for lenders. They quote such verses as: "They are always generous and lend freely; their children will be blessed" (Psalm 37:26) and "Good will come to him who is generous and lends freely, who conducts his affairs with justice" (Psalm 112:5).

In addition, they note that Jesus commends the earning of interest in His parables. Therefore, the argument goes, if lending and earning interest are encouraged, how can borrowing be wrong? After all, you can't have a lender without a borrower, and God would never encourage us to do that which is wrong or unwise.

This argument is built on two fallacies, which can be answered with the following arguments:

1. *The fact that God commends lending does not mean He encourages borrowing.* That would be like saying, "Because God encourages us to feed the hungry, it's good to be starving," or, "Because we are commanded to visit prisons, it must be good to be a prisoner." Yes, it's true that lending to those who are poor and destitute is a righteous thing to do. "He who is kind to the poor lends to the Lord, and he will reward him for what he has done" (Proverbs 19:17).

   But Christian lending should conform to the New Testament admonitions of Christ Himself, a point that most modern lenders prefer to overlook. Jesus said:

   > If you lend to those from whom you expect repayment, what credit is that to you? Even "sinners" lend to "sinners," expecting to be repaid in full. But love your enemies, do good to them, and *lend to them without expecting to get anything back.* Then your reward will be great, and you will be sons of the Most High, because he is kind to the ungrateful and wicked. (Luke 6:34–35; italics added)

   The "lending" Jesus advocated was actually *giving*—expecting nothing back, especially not interest.

2. *Mosaic lending regulations do not encourage borrowing.* In the Old Testament God gave guidelines for many things that believers consider undesirable or downright bad. For example, divorce (Deuteronomy 24) and slavery (Deuteronomy 23) are regulated in the Law, but are not commended as beneficial or healthy practices. Unlike the practice of lending, borrowing is *never* commended or encouraged in Scripture. The opposite is true—the Bible *always* presents borrowing as something to avoid.

Argument 4: The Bible recommends borrowing because Elisha told a widow to borrow jars.

Response: This story, while a valuable lesson for families, is not a ministry model for using borrowed money.

Second Kings 4:1–7 tells the story of a prophet's widow. Her husband had died in debt, and her two sons were about to be taken as slaves by the prophet's creditor. Desperate for help, the widow came to Elisha. Elisha told her to gather as many jars as possible from her neighbors and begin pouring the last of her meager supply of oil into the jars. The oil flowed until every jar she had gathered was filled. When the widow reported this to Elisha, the prophet told her to sell the oil, pay off her debts, and live on the money that was left over.

Using this argument to support ministry borrowing is weak at best, for a couple important reasons:

1. This story has nothing to do with funding corporate ministry (unlike the biblical examples previously cited in this chapter). It's the story of an individual family.

2. The widow was instructed to borrow only objects, not any form of currency or negotiable goods. God provided through the widow's faith and hard work —the jars were probably very big and heavy. The jars were simply tools. This book does not teach against borrowing a neighbor's tool to help you meet your family's financial needs. For example, you might borrow a friend's ax to cut down a tree so you can sell the firewood. That's perfectly biblical. However, if you lose the ax, you'd better be concerned (refer to 2 Kings 6:5).

Argument 5: Forbidding people to borrow is legalistic.

Response: Although we take an admittedly conservative position, we do not advocate "forbidding" anyone to borrow. It's *not a sin* to borrow within the context of ministry, but it is unnecessarily risky.

Some tell us that our non-borrowing ministry position is legalistic. They say that non-borrowing ministry places upon them requirements for righteous living that are not found in the Bible. These folks often quote Galatians 5:1, which says, "It is for freedom that Christ has set us free. Stand firm, then, and do not let yourselves be burdened again by a yoke of slavery." They claim that operating without borrowing places a ministry in slavery to something God doesn't require; hence, "legalism." They sometimes conclude their argument by quoting Matthew 23 and warning us against becoming modern-day Pharisees: "[Woe to you Pharisees who] tie up heavy loads and put them on men's shoulders . . ." (v. 4).

We're not implying that salvation depends upon whether or not someone borrows money for ministry. However, we are saying that non-borrowing ministry conforms to the biblical guidelines for funding ministry. The issue is not one of "legalism" but of *conforming to biblical principles.*

Like any other ministry objective, if it's done with the wrong motives, non-borrowing ministry can become prideful and legalistic. And if by not borrowing you are trying to impress God or surpass the spirituality of others, then you're behaving like a Pharisee.

On the other hand, if non-borrowing ministry is done from a pure heart, for the right motives, it is no more legalistic than conforming to any other principle taught in Scripture.

Argument 6: We can win the lost by borrowing, so it must be within God's will.

Response: Simply because God *allows* us to do things does not mean He *desires* us to do them. The end does not justify the means, and, in the case of borrowing, God has warned us about the means.

It's always dangerous to base a conclusion on a false premise. Unfortunately, that's exactly what this argument does. It is incorrect to believe that a ministry that disregards biblical principles will experience God's highest blessings. As we have seen, God's pattern for funding ministry in the Bible is always "borrow-free." To follow God's ministry pattern means no borrowing. Does the fact that we avoid borrowing mean that we win fewer people to Christ? Will ministering without borrowing slow our growth? Will a "no-borrow" policy cause our ministry, as some have suggested, "to stagnate and die?"[10] Absolutely not! It is *never* a mistake to follow biblical patterns and principles.

There is no guarantee that loan-funded ministries will win more people to Christ. Yes, it's true that larger sanctuaries, better facilities, and more staff can often generate bigger ministries. But bigger is not always best. And the end, no matter how desirable, does not justify the means. How many more people might a ministry win to Christ if that ministry *follows the biblical pattern* and allows God to supernaturally provide the necessary funds through His people?

We need to see *more* evidence of the supernatural working of God in our world, not less. "Borrow-free" ministry is an ideal way for God to demonstrate His faithfulness and power. We believe that God is waiting to pour out His spiritual blessing on ministries that are willing to trust Him completely—especially in their financial matters. As He tells us in 2 Chronicles, "the eyes of the Lord move to and fro throughout the earth that He may strongly support those whose heart is completely His" (16:9 NASB).

Let's do God's work, in God's way, with God's funds, as supplied by His people. Then let's see what happens. Only God knows the blessings we might otherwise miss.

Argument 7: Borrowing is an act of faith.

Response: Of all the arguments that favor ministry borrowing, we hear this one most often. Yet borrowing is actually the *opposite* of faith.

Somehow, a powerful misconception seems to pervade the thinking of many ministries: The idea that it is a step of faith to borrow money. We believe the Bible teaches exactly the opposite. *It is not faith to test God's goodness with presumption.* It is not faith to depend on a lending institution instead of upon God's own supernatural provision.

Those who say borrowing is an act of faith tell us, "It takes faith to pay back a loan." Some go a step further and say, "The larger the loan and the less the collateral, the greater the faith." The ultimate extension of this thinking says, "The largest possible loan with the least possible amount of collateral reflects the greatest amount of faith." However, this viewpoint contradicts every biblical caution about borrowing, and it is dangerously similar to the reasoning of the man who built a tower without counting the cost and then couldn't afford to finish (Luke 14:28–30).

Please don't misunderstand us: Borrowing money doesn't necessarily mean you haven't counted the cost of discipleship. Nor does borrowing automatically indicate that you are guilty of greed. But borrowing usually *does* reflect presumption—believing we know God's will in the future without proof of God's provision in the present.

Some say, "But when you wait until you have all the money in hand before you proceed, that's not walking by faith—it's walking by sight." This argument ignores the clear teaching of the scriptural examples presented in this chapter. *Accumulating funds in advance of ministry is God's very own method!* In stark contrast to the principle of trusting God to supply through His people, the concept of trusting God to help repay loans has no scriptural support whatsoever.

When ministries borrow, they obligate God to provide in the future what He has not made available in the present. *This thinking is presumption, not faith.* Greater risk does not always result in greater faith. Greater risk may very well indicate greater foolishness, as in a round of "Russian roulette." As Larry Burkett has said, "Some people borrow and get away with it. Others get obliterated by debt. Do we really want to put God's church at such risk?"[11] Ministering without borrowing, as God supplies through His people, neither obligates God nor presumes on an ideal future. If borrowing is truly a way of trusting God, why do churches that borrow sometimes end up in bankruptcy? Has God failed?

The richness of the concept of faith is described throughout the Bible in many ways, including: righteousness (Isaiah 26:2; Romans 4:5), an agent in justification (Romans 3:25), and an agent in sanctification (Acts 26:18), as well as the assurance of hope and the certainty of the unseen (Hebrews 11:1). However, none of the 246 verses in the NIV Bible that refer to faith deals with any sort of "faith" that trusts God to make loan payments.

NOTES

1. John MacArthur, "Acts 1–12," in *The MacArthur New Testament Commentary* (Chicago: Moody, 1994), 88.

2. Josephus, *Antiquities* XX.ii.5.

3. Murray Harris, "II Corinthians," in *The Expositor's Bible Commentary,* ed. Frank Gaebelein (Grand Rapids: Zondervan, 1976), vol. 10, 366.

4. Francis Brown, S. R. Driver, and C. A. Briggs, *A Hebrew and English Lexicon of the Old Testament* (1907; reprint Oxford, England: Clarendon Press, 1974), 605.

5. Ibid., 431.

6. Kim Alexander, personal interview, 9 April 1995.

7. Larry Burkett, "Money Matters" radio program, 17 September 1991.

8. W. E. Vine, *An Expository Dictionary of New Testament Words* (Old Tappan, N.J.: Revell, 1940), 50.

9. John F. Walvoord, *Philippians: Triumph in Christ* (Chicago: Moody, 1971), 112.

10. Sherman S. Smith, *Exploding the Doomsday Money Myths* (Nashville: Thomas Nelson, 1994), 109.

11. Burkett, "Money Matters" radio program, 1989.

"Are we glad to hear that you don't know where you'll get the money for the building fund! For a minute there we were afraid you wanted to get it from us."

CHAPTER 5

STRATEGIES FOR BECOMING DEBT-FREE
For Ministries in Debt: Practical Ways to Help Reach Financial Freedom

F ew ministries set out with the objective of going into
debt. Yet far too many churches eventually find themselves in varying degrees of financial bondage.

If your ministry is in financial bondage, you have every
right to be concerned. If your ministry has borrowed money, it has become the servant to a lender, and it is at the
beck and call of its master. You are wise to want to follow
biblical ministry models and avoid borrowing. Yet, as we
have already pointed out, the financial bondage that results from borrowing and debt is most often a self-inflicted
ailment. And like the effort it took to contract the illness,
the cure also requires action.

MOVING TOWARD FINANCIAL FREEDOM: SPECIFIC STRATEGIES

In the course of our experience and research, we have
learned of many ministries that were once in debt but are
no longer. How did those ministries achieve financial freedom? What methods did they use? How did they approach
the problem? What principles did they follow? This chapter is our attempt to answer those questions.

We have identified fifteen scriptural, practical, and creative strategies to employ when trying to move a ministry from dependence on borrowing to dependence on God's sovereign provision. However, this chapter is not a cookbook—it contains no detailed recipes. This information is intended to be an idea generator, a list of alternatives to alert you to strategies you may not have considered.

We're not suggesting that every ministry should use every one of these approaches. Not all of these suggestions will fit your ministry's style. Rather, we suggest you use this information as you would a grocery list: Read over the list and check off the items you feel you can use. (Of course, some items on the list are as crucial to every church's ministry as bread is to a shopping list.) Take the ideas you have marked and apply them with all the excellence you can muster. With God's blessing, your ministry will someday experience the joy of being completely debt-free.

Prayer and/or Fasting

God wants His people to be financially free (Deuteronomy 28; Luke 16). The first effort of the Christian must be prayer. Too often believers relegate prayer to second-class status—something to "try" when all human efforts have been exhausted. Yet prayer is the church's most powerful resource.

Are you wondering where to start? These suggestions are by no means all-inclusive, but we recommend you specifically bring several requests before the Father:

- Pray that God will work in the hearts of your ministry leaders to impress them with the importance of having a Bible-based, debt-free conviction.

- Pray that He will make you, your leaders, and your people open and receptive to His leading—whatever that may be.

- Pray that God will help the process of becoming debt-free to be one of unity and harmony, rather than division and dissension.

- Pray that God will touch the hearts of His people and open the floodgates of His abundant provision through their giving.

Prayer is powerful (James 5:16). Start your debt-free initiative with prayer and bathe it constantly in prayer. And for those who feel called to do so, try fasting. But whether through prayer alone or by prayer and fasting, bring your needs before God. He hears and answers (Psalm 91:15).

Commitment from Leadership

People will follow if a ministry's leaders are men of integrity who set the proper example. But it's unrealistic to expect people to do what ministry leaders are unwilling to do. Leadership attitude, commitment, and example all play a vital role in the process of becoming financially free.

Ministry leaders need to see borrowing and lending as God sees it (Proverbs 22:7). To the lender, it's empowerment. To the borrower, it's enslavement. For ministries to set the example, ministry leaders must first be convinced.

One additional point to consider is the personal financial situation of your ministry leaders, who need to be exemplary models of Christian thinking and living. Although there is no biblical command for ministry leaders to be debt-free, the Scripture is clear that they need to be wise managers of their personal finances. Refer to chapters 4 and 7 for more information about the role of ministry leadership in becoming debt-free.

Scriptural Giving

Throughout this book we stress the critical importance of generous giving. Without an abundance of joyful, sacrificial gifts from God's people, it's exceedingly difficult for a ministry to be financially free. Sadly, most ministries borrow primarily because God's people refuse to give in a scriptural manner. Yet *all* believers need to financially support their local churches through regular, biblical giving.

Individual believers must be willing to sacrifice personal luxuries and non-necessities for the benefit of the body corporate. Only then will ministries become financially free.

A Written Plan

The Bible instructs believers, "Make plans by seeking advice; if you wage war, obtain guidance" (Proverbs 20:18). In Proverbs 21:5, God says, "The plans of the diligent lead to profit as surely as haste leads to poverty."

In the same way a calendar is a vital part of successful time management, an effective plan must be an important part of your efforts to become a debt-free ministry. Don't be afraid to ask for advice; you're trying to "wage war" against the monster of financial bondage, and you need advice and guidance to win. We suggest you contact one of the ministries listed at the end of this chapter. All of them expressed a desire to help others, and you'll be encouraged when you speak with people who have been where you are.

Get the input and advice you need for the strategies you want to use, then build a written plan to implement those strategies and avoid further borrowing. Without a written plan, you may never reach your goals. But with a written plan and measurable, achievable objectives, you have a much better opportunity for success.

Loan Prepayment

Have your accountant run the numbers. You'll see that your ministry can save many thousands (or tens of thousands) of dollars over the life of a loan by prepaying (assuming your loan agreement allows prepayment). The sooner you pay off your loan and the less you pay, the more resources can be freed up for true ministry.

Don't be discouraged if you think you can't prepay very much—even a small amount extra each month can result in surprisingly substantial savings over time.

No Additional Borrowing

As Larry Burkett says, "If you don't borrow any more money, you won't get any deeper in debt." That's a true and powerful statement (assuming, of course, that you are paying the bills on time and making your required payments in full). You will get out of debt much more quickly if you stop borrowing altogether.

Consider the example of Northwest Community Church in Phoenix, Arizona. When Jay Letey was called as senior pastor, he nearly refused. The church of a few thousand was experiencing extreme financial difficulties and was on the verge of bankruptcy. Having borrowed to buy land, the ministry was $5 million in debt. At one time the church's indebtedness consumed a full *90 percent* of its monthly income.

By the time Letey visited Northwest to explore the call to ministry, the previous pastor had resigned and many staff members had been laid off. Some accounts payable were behind as much as 120 days. Finances were so tight that at one point the church literally could not afford to print bulletins.

After much prayer, Letey accepted the call. But he agreed to come only because the congregation had established and met the following non-negotiable conditions:

1. The church had stopped all borrowing and had purposed to never borrow again.
2. Every active person in the church had assumed ownership of ministry tasks, since staff could no longer be hired.
3. The church had humbly approached its creditors and was negotiating a mutually agreeable yet manageable loan repayment schedule.
4. The congregation was trying to sell the unused portion of the church's property, with the goal of putting the entire proceeds of the sale against the indebtedness.
5. The ministry had committed to living within its means on a week-by-week basis.

Since 1988, the church has stayed true to its non-borrowing commitment. The ministry's loan balance has been reduced to $1.2 million, and some of the staff positions have been restored. The church is experiencing conservative but steady growth, and people are excited about the ministry.

So if your ministry has a need, take comfort! God will meet that need through the generous gifts of His people (2 Corinthians 9:6–15). And if He doesn't sovereignly supply what you need, *don't borrow.* Learn to live without and still be content (Philippians 4:10–13).

The Involvement of Everyone

There are more than enough resources in the body of Christ to accomplish everything that God wants to do. Yet American Christians indulge themselves while much of God's work goes unfunded or underfunded.

Many legitimate comparisons can be made between the modern American church and the situation described by the prophet Haggai in Jerusalem in 520 B.C. Instead of rebuilding the temple, as they should have been doing, they were "busy" living in richly appointed homes. Yet because they were not involved in God's work, they suffered from significant economic hardships.

Debt-free ministry is virtually impossible unless everyone participates, contributing not only their finances, but their time, their talents, their training, and their spiritual gifts. Debt-free ministry is everyone's responsibility, and *everyone* must get involved. For example, both Circle Community Church and Spirit Lake Baptist Church report significant cost benefits from constructing modest debt-free buildings with their own congregations as the primary labor source.

The "Smallest First" Loan Repayment Strategy

When Christian Financial Concepts trains family financial counselors, one aspect of their training is to help people strategize debt repayment. One particularly valuable tactic in becoming debt-free is the "smallest first" repayment strategy. If your ministry is repaying several loans, this approach may be of significant benefit to you.

The concept is simple: Concentrate surplus resources on paying off the smallest loan balance. When the smallest loan is paid off, take all the money that was being paid against it and add that to the amount you're paying on the next-smallest loan. When that loan is paid off, tackle the third-smallest loan in the same way, and so on.

This is exactly the method used by Harvest Christian Fellowship after their 1993 "Tithing Revival" resulted in dramatically increased giving. According to Pastor John Sonneland, the church was debt-free in less than eighteen months.

Note that as the smallest loan balances have been paid off and you face the larger amounts, it may be financially wiser to shift your focus toward paying off loans with higher interest rates. Have your accountant calculate your most advantageous payoff sequence.

Spending Cuts

When you reduce spending, you can apply more money to paying off loans. And because of the multiplying power of compound interest, even a small prepayment can save much down the road.

So try to spend less. We're not suggesting you cut back your missions budget or pastoral salaries. Rather, we're encouraging you to identify *unneeded* or *overfunded* budget categories and reduce or eliminate them. You may be able to put certain non-essential programs "on hold" until after your loans are paid off. Remember: If your ministry doesn't control its spending, spending will control your ministry.

Of course, this presupposes your ministry has a carefully crafted budget. An excellent, godly budget is a minimum requirement for ministries that want to be wise managers of God's resources. The Scripture says, "Be sure you know the condition of your flocks, give careful attention to your herds" (Proverbs 27:23). Wise budgeting skills are just as important for ministries as they are for families.

Sale of Assets

For debt-free ministry to be a reachable goal, individual believers must be willing to sacrifice their resources. Ministries must also be willing to liquidate unneeded resources. The proceeds from the sale of ministry-owned real estate, buildings, excess supplies, and other resources can be used to move your ministry to financial freedom much more quickly than you may have thought.

Both Circle Community Church and Fellowship Bible Church have used this strategy, with notable success. When Circle Community was building a new auditorium (without borrowing) in 1986, the church raised a significant portion of the funds it needed by selling an unused, undeveloped North Carolina vacation lot that had been donated to the church years before.

As this manuscript was being prepared, Fellowship was in the process of raising the funds for a $1.2 million non-borrowing building project. To augment the congregational giving, the elders were selling two unneeded residential properties that had been donated to the ministry.

Cooperation with Other Ministries

Seventh-Day Adventist congregations across America are generously sharing their facilities with non-Adventist churches. The Adventist congregation meets on Saturday, and the non-Adventist group meets on Sunday. Some details can present an administrative problem (for example, hymnal and Sunday-school materials storage for the non-Adventist congregation). Midweek services may require creative or nontraditional scheduling. But all these minor challenges can easily be overcome with love, unity, respect, and flexibility.

Due to the escalating costs of facilities, cooperative ministry efforts that were once thought unusual are becoming increasingly common. Here are just two examples of how churches and parachurch ministries—such as mission boards—are learning to cut costs and increase facilities usage by coexisting in the same physical plant:

- The Home Mission Board of the Southern Baptist Convention is sharing its new national office building in Alpharetta, Georgia, with a newly formed congregation. The Church at North Point will meet in the HMB building's 500-seat multi-purpose room.
- In Maitland, Florida, the Orlando campus of Reformed Theological Seminary shares its facilities

with the congregation of Orlando Grace Church. The seminary recently announced plans to relocate from its current leased facilities to its own new campus in the nearby town of Oviedo. When the campus moves, the church will relocate along with it.

This kind of obvious, outward cooperation among believers builds Christian unity. And as Christ prayed before He went to the cross, Christian unity is what demonstrates both His deity and God's love to a lost and searching world (John 17:21–23).

Fund-Raising Events

This is suggested only for ministries that feel the freedom to do so. Bake sales, car washes, church-wide garage sales, candy sales, and so forth can potentially raise a significant amount of money for loan repayment.

Here's an important caution: Be sure your ministry has dealt aggressively and appropriately with the root causes for its financial bondage. As with individuals who have lost their financial freedom, borrowing is not the problem; it's but a symptom of the real problems, which are usually spiritual in nature. Additional income is normally not the best way to deal with financial bondage. Unless the individual or ministry expresses a firm conviction against further borrowing, increased income simply becomes the means to justify a new loan payment.

So be sure the real ministry problems are being fixed as a part of your journey toward financial freedom. If the root causes go unresolved, no amount of additional income will release a ministry from financial bondage.

Innovative Giving Opportunities

We encourage you to think outside of the box that regular ministry practice and custom sometimes force you into. This can be especially significant when developing opportunities for people to give. God has decreed few specific ministry methods; and the same old, tired methods of the past can be increasingly ineffective as we approach the next millennium. In proper context, new ideas can spark tremendous response.

For example, remember the "Joash" system used by Denton Bible Church with its "Heave-Ho for Cold Cash" ice chest. Over time, Denton has raised a total of $1.5 million in this unusual way.

Fellowship Bible Church's effort to build a new debt-free facility has resulted in several unique approaches to stimulate giving. One idea was a "Give a Brick for Christmas" campaign, which encouraged people to buy bricks for the new building at fifty cents each. At the end of this creative holiday giving opportunity, Fellowship had collected enough money to buy all thirty thousand bricks needed for the new facility.

Open Communication

Effective, open communication throughout the ministry is vital to the success of a debt-free initiative. Try to maximize the efficiency of all ministry communication tools, including prayer networks, bulletins, newsletters, congregational meetings, ministry leaders' meetings, cottage meetings, printed information, budget calculations, and any other methods you use to communicate within your ministry.

Clear communication of ministry needs played a significant role in the giving that resulted from those needs being shared. People tend to support what they know about, what they understand, what they agree with, and what ministry leaders say is important. Work to ensure open, free-flowing communication so people can be knowledgeable and responsive contributors to your debt-free plan.

Teaching, Training, and Counseling

The church needs to be at the forefront of training people to manage the resources God has entrusted to them. Fortunately we live in a day in which such training is readily available. There are small-group Bible studies; seminars; adult, teen, and children's instructional materials, books, and workbooks; videotaped lecture series; one-on-one counseling programs; and much more.

If your ministry doesn't provide any of these teaching resources, it may be very difficult to combat the overwhelming impact of today's debt-fueled culture. People need to have their debt-free convictions firmly grounded in the Word of God.

Refer to the appendix for a list of financial ministry contacts, such as Christian Financial Concepts, Crown Ministries, and other helpful organizations and resources. Get the support you need to bring solid, biblical financial teaching into your ministry. Who knows? You may be the one God uses to help your ministry develop a strong, debt-free conviction.

Trusting God to Provide

Someone has said of God's sovereign provision that "He is seldom early but never late." However, when people refuse to exercise their faith, God looks elsewhere for those who are committed to trusting Him. Second Chronicles 16:9 says that "the eyes of the Lord range throughout the earth to strengthen those whose hearts are fully committed to him."

Scripture is replete with God's promises to meet our needs. The Bible provides many examples of how God generously supplies the needs of ministry. However, the Father often supplies in unusual ways, ways that are sometimes not apparent to our limited perceptions. The question is: *Do we really trust God* to supply all our needs?

Larry Burkett tells the thought-provoking story about his personal experience with a church whose need had been met, but didn't know it. Because the ministry did not trust *completely* in God's provision, it ended up in financial bondage:

> A few years back God allowed me to observe how a credit mind-set can cause us to miss out on God's best. A Christian businessman I knew came to my office for counsel. He'd made a large profit in a real estate transaction and wanted to give much of it to the Lord's work. His church was building a youth center and he wanted to give all the money to that project. But he had a very strong conviction against borrowing money in general, and specifically against his church borrowing money to build that building.

He said to me, "I'll give the church all the money for the building if you can convince the pastor to build it debt-free, without him knowing about my gift." Well, what a dilemma that was! The pastor and I were good friends so I asked him and one of his deacons to meet me for lunch.

At that meal I did everything I could do within the restrictions placed on me to convince the pastor to make an absolute commitment to build the youth center debt-free. I thought I was making some headway with arguments like, "Don't stifle God's ability to bless your people" and "If you can't trust God for the money you need, do you really trust God?"

Because the pastor and I were friends, I knew he basically wanted to build the youth center debt-free. He was even willing to do so, provided his church board supported it. But at the very end of our conversation the pastor asked his deacon (a local businessman) what he thought of our discussion. The deacon replied, "If I tried to run my business by the principles Larry just outlined, I'd be broke today. And if we try to build this building debt-free, our kids are going to be grown and gone before the walls are up. It's a great theory, Pastor, but it just won't work today."

The pastor caved in under the deacon's reasoning. He walked away from our lunch meeting with a commitment to borrow the money from a local bank; and he intended to present his plan to the congregation that evening. As he left I wanted to shout, "But if you'll believe God, the money is already there!" Of course, I couldn't because I had promised not to.

The next day my businessman friend told me he'd given his check to another ministry—a check for over $200,000. The church went on to borrow the money. They've been paying on that loan for about ten years now and they'll continue to pay for almost another twenty years. It's interesting that everything they needed was already provided by God. All they had to do was trust Him for it.[1]

God *will* meet our ministry needs. All He asks is that we trust Him.

FINANCIALLY FREE MINISTRIES YOU CAN CONTACT

The dream of being financially free is a reality to many healthy, growing ministries across America. Non-borrowing ministries can be found in many denominations and geographical areas. Most of the ministries listed in this section were once in financial bondage but are no longer. Several of these ministries have never borrowed money for any reason. One of them is still repaying its obligations, but moving steadily toward financial freedom. All of them expressed a willingness to share their stories with others.

If you feel the need to contact a debt-free ministry for input, information, and encouragement, we suggest you contact the ministries on this list.

1. *Denton Bible Church,* 1910 East University Avenue, Denton, TX 76201 (2,500 in attendance, twenty years old, debt-free for nine years)

2. *Covenant Presbyterian Church,* 720 Emerson Drive, Palm Bay, FL 32907 (700 in attendance, seventeen years old, debt-free for three years)

3. *Fellowship Bible Church,* 806 Walnut Avenue, Dalton, GA 30720 (350 in attendance, twenty-four years old, debt-free for thirteen years)

4. *Frazier Memorial United Methodist Church,* 6000 Atlanta Highway, Montgomery, AL 36117 (4,500 in attendance, twenty-eight years old, debt-free for three years)

5. *Glenfield Baptist Church,* 670 South Lambert Road, Glen Ellyn, IL 60137 (150 in attendance, thirty-two years old, debt-free for thirteen years)

6. *Grace Bible Fellowship,* Valley Road, Box 651B, Walpole, NH 03608 (100 in attendance, thirteen years old, always debt-free)

7. *Harvest Christian Fellowship,* 1316 North Lincoln Street, Spokane, WA 99201 (800 in attendance, twenty-four years old, debt-free for two years)

8. *Northwest Community Church,* 16615 North Forty-third Avenue, Phoenix, AZ 85023 (1,500 in attendance, thirty-eight years old, has been moving toward financial freedom for seven years)

9. *Prince Avenue Baptist Church,* P.O. Box 1112, Athens, GA 30603 (1,100 in attendance, eighty-four years old, debt-free for twenty-one years)

10. *RBC Ministries,* 3000 Kraft Avenue Southeast, Grand Rapids, MI 49512 (fifty-seven years old, always debt-free)

11. *Spirit Lake Baptist Church,* P.O. Box 587, Spirit Lake, ID 83869 (90 in attendance, eight years old, debt-free for six years)

NOTE

1. Larry Burkett, "Money Matters" radio program, 30 July 1991.

CHAPTER 6

STRATEGIES FOR
DEBT-FREE MINISTRY EXPANSION
Remaining Debt-Free While Growing Your Ministry

Ministries borrow money for many reasons, such as to build, remodel, develop new programs and outreaches, or even to supplement budget shortfalls. However, building is the most common reason for ministry borrowing. Many of you are reading this book because your church or ministry is thinking about borrowing to build—and you're looking for answers. This chapter is directed primarily toward growing, debt-free ministries that want to continue growing while remaining financially free.

This chapter offers a range of biblical alternatives to conventional borrowing—alternatives you may not have known about or previously considered. According to Larry Burkett, "Ninety percent of all church building programs include indebtedness."[1] And if your ministry is thinking of building, you're not alone. It's an issue that must be faced by most American ministries at some point. Consider these 1994 church statistics:

- 94 percent of America's churches own a building, 83 percent have a parking lot, 54 percent have a parsonage, and 32 percent own a garage or other outbuilding.

- 68 percent have engaged in a major renovation of their building at some time in their history (32 percent within the past four years).

- 67 percent have built an addition to their building at some time in their history (15 percent within the last four years).

- 30 percent plan a major renovation in the near future (19 percent within the next year and a half).

- 29 percent plan to build an addition in the near future (13 percent within the next year and a half).[2]

More than one-fourth of America's churches currently have a building-related fund-raising program in place or plan to start one soon.[3] The question is, "How will this ministry expansion be funded?"

THE FOUNDATIONS FOR DEBT-FREE MINISTRY

Let's say your ministry is growing. Souls are being won to Christ. Disciples are being built up in their faith. Others are being helped, trained, and encouraged. Your people are excited about the ministry and involved in its work. But your current facilities seem to be at the limits of their capacity. If your ministry is a church, you're afraid people will start attending elsewhere rather than "fight" for a parking place or a seat. Or maybe you don't need to build—you may simply want to branch out into a new area of ministry, but the money doesn't seem to be there.

How will you fund your expansion? Will you borrow money? Consider this challenging statement from Larry Burkett: "The way a church raises and administers its money is an outer reflection of an inner conviction. Our faith grows stronger when it's tried and tested (James 1:3–4). This certainly applies to our faith in regard to finances."[4]

Perhaps the single most important factor to consider when thinking about ministry expansion is: *Who will get the credit?* For example, when you borrow to build, the lender usually gets the credit. In fact, a sign often goes up in front of the property that proclaims: "Financing by First

Federal Bank." But when the provision for ministry expansion comes directly from God—through the generous, sacrificial giving of His people—only *He* can get the credit.

Before embarking on a non-borrowing ministry expansion, make sure you have carefully thought through several foundational issues: your purpose, your mission, and your plan.

Purpose

Before expanding your ministry, you need to first answer the question "why?" *Why* are you expanding your ministry? What is your purpose? The overriding purpose of all Christian ministry must be to *glorify God.* "So whether you eat or drink or whatever you do, do it all for the glory of God" (1 Corinthians 10:31). Before you start, be *certain* that you're not expanding your ministry by human effort or for selfish reasons.

The Great Commission of Jesus Christ is a mandate to make disciples, *not* to build buildings. Facilities and programs are only tools that can sometimes help in the process of reaching people. Christian organizations too often become facility-driven or program-driven, rather than being ministry-driven. Countless dollars and endless hours—not to mention a ministry's real God-given purpose—are often lost in exhausting efforts to maintain and expand facilities and programs.

Mission

The second issue to address before expanding your ministry is "what?" *What* do you intend to do? Have you clearly identified your specific ministry targets? Can you succinctly describe exactly what your ministry is trying to accomplish? Too often ministries unwittingly place a higher priority on human activity than on clear direction from God.

We recommend you develop a clearly worded philosophy of ministry that unites purpose (why?) and mission (what?) into one coherent statement. Many excellent books can help you think through and construct an effective mission statement. Visit your local Christian bookstore (or even your local library) for more information.

Plan

A third vital issue to address before expanding your ministry is "how?" *How* will your purpose and philosophy be put into practice? What methods will you use? What are your specific objectives, and when do you plan to reach them? How will you measure your success?

For example, does your ministry have a five-year plan? Both long- and short-range plans are important for any organization's ultimate success. Careful planning is especially important if a ministry wants to build. Any building or other ministry expansion should result from and fit into that ministry's overall strategic plan. This isn't a book on strategic planning, and we're not going to explain planning details. However, planning is right, good, wise, scriptural, and vital for true success.

We're not suggesting you make legalistic, rigid plans that are closed to revision as God's Spirit moves in the hearts of people. The scriptural perspective on planning can be summed up like this: Write your plans in pencil—then give God the eraser.

If you have doubts about God's perspective on planning, study these key Scriptures that address the wisdom and importance of planning:

- Building the tabernacle was the outworking of *plans* from God Himself. In Exodus 26:30 God instructed Moses to "Set up the tabernacle according to the *plan* shown you on the mountain."
- David made specific *plans* for building the temple (1 Chronicles 28:2–19).
- A wealth of Bible passages speak highly of godly *plans,* including Psalm 20:4; Proverbs 12:5; 14:22; 15:22; 16:3, 9; 20:18; 21:5; Isaiah 32:8; Jeremiah 29:11; and 2 Corinthians 1:15–17.

Effective planning yields remarkable ministry benefits: It defines an organization's purpose, authenticates its mission, identifies known expectations, describes apparent limitations, establishes specific goals, and sets measurable objectives. If your ministry expansion or building objectives are part of efficient ministry planning, we recommend that you study the alternatives for expansion that are described in this chapter. If after all things are considered you're confident that God wants you to move, then move.

But if wise and careful planning reveals that your ministry cannot expand or build without borrowing, we recommend you put your plans on hold. It's wise to delay expansion until God provides the necessary funding through the generous giving of His people. Waiting on the Lord is *never* a problem; running ahead of God *always* is.

GOD'S FUNDING METHOD

When the time comes to fund ministry expansion, too many ministry leaders immediately call a bond company or make an appointment with a commercial loan officer at the bank. Why do ministries so frequently borrow to fund expansion? In many cases, they feel they have no alternatives. Far too often, they don't even *look* for alternatives.

But it doesn't have to be that way. There are solid alternatives to bonds and banks. In addition to the useful ministry strategies we presented in chapter 5, we've identified fifteen scriptural, practical, and creative strategies for expanding a ministry without borrowing.

Not all of these strategies are intended for every ministry. You'll need to carefully evaluate each strategy for its appropriateness to your ministry style and culture.

Biblical, Generous, and Sacrificial Giving

In his pamphlet *Should Churches Borrow?* Larry Burkett makes this bold assertion: "It's a fact that most of the building programs and ministry outreaches that are truly needed could be funded by the Christians involved surrendering less than ten percent of their savings. They don't, either because of a lack of commitment or because borrowing is an easy alternative."[5] Study after study shows that most Christians give little to their churches, forcing pastors and church boards into what author and teacher Henry Blackaby calls "a crisis of belief." Convinced that their people will not give, church leaders too often feel trapped and resort to borrowing out of a sense of desperation.

Christians need to give in a generous, joyous, God-first, servant-minded, self-sacrificial way, in proportion to their incomes. *If Christians would give as God clearly instructs them to, there would never be a need for ministries to borrow.*

Yet when challenged to give up personal desires in favor of contributing to the work and expansion of churches and ministries, too many American Christians say no. This is *not* the giving attitude that is powerfully and consistently taught throughout the New Testament.

How does God want to fund the New Testament church? Not through borrowing or bonds—but through the generous giving of His very own people. *Liberal giving is the single most fundamental aspect of ministry that enables financial freedom.*

Whether we live in fabulous wealth or abject poverty, we are commanded to place our faith and hope not in material things, but in God Himself (1 Timothy 6:7; James 2:5). Our faithful God will supply everything that He wants His people to have—and to give—both spiritually and physically. Being content with what God has given, giving generously, and spending only from what is left—without borrowing— is the key to getting past the worldly complaint that no income is ever quite high enough. God will provide the needs of the faithful believer.

Remember how the tabernacle was built (Exodus 35–36)? The principles of giving for ministry expansion—or any other purpose—are really no different today: Ministry leaders should teach God's Word, and God's people should get their hearts right. When asked to give, believers should give according to what they have purposed in their hearts before God. People who are fully committed to God will give with such generosity that they will need to be told when to stop!

One of the most common reasons that ministry leaders cite when borrowing to expand ministry is "Our people would/could never give that kind of money!" It may sound harsh, but this question can be legitimately raised of a ministry that does not practice biblical, generous, and sacrificial giving: Are your people *spiritually mature enough* to effectively deal with the increased responsibility and accountability that results from an expanded ministry?

The bottom line? Sacrificial giving is the *foundation* of God's system for performing, expanding, and completing ministry. For more details about biblical giving, refer to chapter 9.

EXPANDING MINISTRY WITHOUT BORROWING

What if your church members give generously, but you still cannot currently support a building program, which it seems you need desperately? The reasons could be numerous: past financial errors, a high unemployment rate, or special needs among your missionaries. Regardless of the reason, God has not opened the door for you to build larger facilities. Are there other alternatives that will help you meet your needs without borrowing? Here are several that have worked for other ministries.

Set Up Multiple Services and/or Congregations

In a growing church, multiple services can go a long way toward easing the crunch that often drives a facilities expansion. However, multiple services are more difficult and demanding, and require more effective administration than does a single service. Yet when handled effectively, the use of multiple services can stave off the need to build for a significant amount of time—perhaps even long enough for a generous, giving congregation to raise the money for non-borrowing expansion.

Multiple services often take on different characters, sometimes to the point of becoming completely different congregations (whether by design or otherwise). For example, one "congregation" could attend a more traditional service that is designed to reach people who are more comfortable with hymn-based worship music and a robed choir. Another service could be designed for a different group, perhaps one that prefers modern worship choruses and personal sharing. In this way, two very different "congregations" could use the same facility.

Depending on how innovative and flexible a church is, worship services can be scheduled at various times during the week or throughout the day on Sunday. We must remember that our traditional, denominational formulas (such as Sunday school/worship/training union/Sunday evening) are not found in the Bible. God has clearly defined the purpose and mission of the church, but He has graciously left most of the plans and methods to us.

Is God being glorified by your plans? In other words, are more of His message, His attributes, and His character being revealed to a lost world through your methods? If so, don't be concerned if they are nontraditional. But be sure they are scriptural. Those nontraditional methods may go a long way toward keeping your ministry debt-free.

Rent an Alternative Facility

Renting an alternative facility is an option that many churches can afford. The growing church's problem is often not one of inadequate *cash flow* to meet expenses, but inadequate *cash reserves* to expand. That's where renting comes in. Keep in mind that during the greatest ministry expansion in history—the aftermath of Pentecost—the church had no buildings of its own, but met mostly in homes and sometimes in an "alternative facility"—the temple. Consider these rental possibilities:

- Schools
- Public buildings (such as city or community centers)
- Community-service organizations (women's clubs, Elks clubs, and others)
- Conference, convention, or trade centers
- A Seventh-Day Adventist church or a Jewish synagogue

Some of these options were described in chapter 5. Chapter 5 also explores another alternative-facilities option: sharing facilities with another type of Christian ministry.

Remodel Existing Facilities

This method is one of the most overlooked expansion ideas, but it often bears the most promise. Over time we become so familiar with our existing facilities that we fail to recognize the potential for increased efficiency that often lies untapped right within our own walls.

Ray Bowman says, "Churches that think they are running out of room often are surprised to learn that they can double or triple in size without a major building program simply by changing how they think about and use their present space."[6] Bowman states that "Until a church fully utilizes its existing building, a need for more space does not exist."[7]

Bowman goes on to present a number of ways to restructure for expansion, including matching class size to room size, using furniture effectively, organizing space efficiently, scheduling activities creatively, remodeling, and more.[8] He even devotes an entire chapter of his book to the subject of "Remodeling for Growth." Highly recommended!

Sign a Long-Term Lease

The key advantage to a lease is that a ministry need not lay out a huge amount of cash. Like leasing an apartment, if you can make your monthly lease payment, you can move in. For a rapidly growing ministry, this could be an option. Sometimes you can lease with an option to buy.

Occasionally the lease holder will remodel the facilities to suit your needs before you move in. One congregation in the Orlando area was offered free custom remodeling as an incentive to sign a long-term lease. They accepted.

Purchase a Larger Church Facility

Bank loan officers tell us that when a church is built, the unfortunate but all-too-common result is that the property is worth less than similar commercial property when it's time to sell. Often a growing congregation that wants to sell its property and build elsewhere finds that its existing property has little value—except to another church.

In cases like this, a small but growing church can sometimes purchase everything it needs in one fell swoop. Taking over a larger church can involve no more than changing stationery, business cards, bulletins, telephone listings, and the name on the sign out front. Just be sure you don't take on more space than you can reasonably afford to maintain.

Restructure a Non-Church Facility

Occasionally, restructuring a non-church facility can be an affordable alternative, but be sure to count the cost. Too often this alternative can be as expensive—or more so—as building a new, conventional church building. As with all construction projects, be sure to get detailed estimates from several reputable builders before you start breaking out walls. You might find the overall cost to be prohibitively expensive.

Build It Yourself

When you use the labor of your people to "build it yourself," you can sometimes build for only the cost of materials. Occasionally, even the materials are donated. And the unity and synergy that result from a group of believers constructing their own facility with their own hands can be a dynamic experience in the life of a ministry.

Circle Community Church's auditorium is an excellent example of this point. In 1986, the church owed well over $100,000 from the earlier purchase of its existing facility and property. Because the existing facility was a remodeled commercial site that was less than ideal, the elders developed a plan. They proposed to build a new, larger, multipurpose auditorium to bridge a gap between two buildings they already owned. The congregation was concerned about the thousands of dollars every month that were being paid to the church's mortgage holder, so elders and congregation alike determined to build without additional borrowing.

The Debt-Free Auditorium. The church started a fundraising drive, and about $60,000 was raised in less than a year. When the church had enough money to purchase the needed permits and materials, construction began, with one of the church members (the owner of a construction company) serving as general contractor. Nearly every part of the new facility, from the concrete-block walls to the roof shingles to the air-conditioning installation, was built on a volunteer basis—mostly on weekends.

The unity that sprang from that effort brought the church together as nothing before. The women of the church fed the men as they worked, the children served as laborers, and relationships were born over saws and hammers that endure to this day. The final outcome was a carpeted, air-conditioned, 300-seat multi-purpose auditorium, complete with landscaping, sound system, skylights, and movable-chair seating.

This is the "Oholiab and Bezalel" model for constructing a facility—the "do-it-yourself" plan that God used to build the tabernacle (as recounted in the book of Exodus; specifically chapters 31 and 35–38). The do-it-yourself method could also be called the "Nehemiah" model for facilities renovation. In addition, the Bible gives a detailed description of the important role of donated and recycled materials in the rebuilding of Jerusalem in 445 B.C. (Nehemiah 2–7).

It's great when a building project can help create unity in a ministry, but remember this caution: Be sure your construction project doesn't detract from real ministry. Building a structure is service, but it is *not* ministry—serving people is ministry. In fact, Ray Bowman recommends against the build-it-yourself method. His experience indicates that the effort involved in a congregation doing the construction work itself almost always distracts people from real ministry and ultimately hinders growth. Bowman exhorts churches to commit to the principle of "focus," which he explains as follows: "Our church will build only when we can do so without changing our focus from ministry to building."[9]

Build in Phases

A phased building approach can be an effective way to avoid borrowing. With a phased approach, a ministry builds only as funds are available. When funding stops, building stops.

However, it's important to use the phased approach wisely. Be sure to stop building at an appropriate time. If the phased approach is used unwisely, such problems as weather damage and permit expiration can end up costing your ministry a lot of extra money, time, and inconvenience.

Many of the debt-free churches we interviewed have used a phased building approach. However, be sure to count the cost (Luke 14:28–33). Sometimes phased building projects must sit unfinished for extended periods of time. Be sure to complete your building in such a way that the unfinished appearance of the structure is not a blight on the landscape and a reproach to the name of Christ.

A church in northern Illinois used the phased approach to build a new auditorium —but without careful planning. The church had a dynamic and popular pastor who left the church in the middle of the building project, even before the roof was on the new building. A large part of the congregation followed him to his next church. Construction on the new building stopped. A series of new pastors were unable to revitalize the church, which was plagued with debt problems that had begun even before the new building project.

The result was a dark, hulking, ugly shell of a building that was an embarrassment to the church and the community for years. The church gradually faded away, and eventually the property was purchased by a neighboring supermarket. The building shell was demolished and paved over as a new section of the supermarket parking lot. All that remained of the once-booming facility was the gymnasium, which the supermarket converted into a warehouse.

Build an Inexpensive Metal Building

Many people have negative thoughts when the subject of metal buildings is brought up. However, modern metal buildings are not the plain, boxlike structures many envision. A modern metal building is as attractive, as durable, and as useful as a building of conventional construction, but it can cost up to 50 percent less per square foot to construct. In addition, a metal building can easily be designed to expand to accommodate future growth.

Plant Daughter Churches

Is a megachurch really necessary? This question revisits the issue of planning and vision. Would you rather have several smaller, more intimate churches or a single, large church where it's easier to get lost and avoid relationships?

If God hasn't sovereignly created a large ministry, we suggest you avoid trying to create one yourself. Church-growth gurus disagree about the ideal size a church should be before it can effectively support a healthy daughter church, but we suggest your congregation give this strategy careful consideration.

We believe that healthy ministries must find ways to reproduce themselves throughout their communities. So instead of building a bigger facility, why not build another ministry, in another needy area? This is where many of the creative alternatives in this book can be effectively used to help avoid borrowing. For example, the congregation of a newly planted Presbyterian church could rent facilities from a Seventh-Day Adventist church while the new church is in start-up mode.

Meet in Homes

This alternative to an expensive building project is the primary facilities "plan" for the majority of the world's Christians. However, it is only in recent years that the American church has begun to return to its apostolic roots. For example, Fellowship Bible Church avoids the expense and hassle of a corporate Sunday evening service by having cell-group meetings in homes.

A church can realize impressive benefits when it meets in homes. The intimacy and informality of gathering in a home helps cultivate a sense of belonging, which meets one of the greatest human needs. In addition, people are more willing to share their doubts, fears, and troubles in the presence of a few friends. And when people feel free to speak openly, real ministry can take place.

The issue of ministry focus is a critical consideration when planning to expand or build. A ministry with a "high-touch" focus will often have small groups as a central ministry dynamic, and a personal home is the most friendly, open, and scriptural of small-group environments.

"Portable Church"

There is a company that markets an entire, mobile, modular church "system"—everything a congregation needs, right down to hymnals and nursery toys. After the service, everything is rapidly and neatly packed up into a storage area or a trailer. You set up the "church" wherever there's an open hall or auditorium.

Kensington Community Church of Troy, Michigan, has grown to nearly two thousand people and saved many tens of thousands of dollars with Portable Church's modular, quick set-up and take-down system. For more information about Portable Church, call (810) 879–7887.

SOME IMPORTANT REMINDERS

There are many exciting and creative ways to expand a ministry without borrowing. But it's also true that non-borrowing ministry can be difficult. It's a challenge to do God's work in God's way, and debt-free ministry is no exception. Here are five important reminders to consider as you try to expand a ministry without borrowing:

- It's not easy.
- It can be a slow process (by human standards).
- Other ministries will borrow and seem to prosper.
- The vision must be regularly rekindled.
- By God's grace, ministries can remain debt-free.

LEADERSHIP PLAYS A VITAL ROLE

Non-borrowing ministry is most effective when ministry leadership is at the forefront, clearly championing God's best and highest for His people. And that message rings forth with the greatest conviction when ministry leaders apply "borrow-free" living principles in their own personal affairs. Leaders who themselves avoid borrowing are ideally positioned to cast vision and direction for a non-borrowing ministry.

American Christians are the "rich in this world" that Paul referred to in 1 Timothy 6:17. By any world standard, Americans are fabulously wealthy people. As such, American ministry leaders are commanded by God to command us to "be rich in good deeds, and to be generous and willing to share." In the same letter, Paul gives significant instruction about how a ministry leader should handle his financial affairs: He is not to be a "lover of money" (1 Timothy 3:3). He "must manage his own family well" (v. 4); otherwise, "how can he take care of God's church?" (v. 5). Deacons must not pursue dishonest gain (v. 8), and they must have a firm grasp of the "deep truths of the faith" (v. 9).

One of the deepest truths of the Christian faith is that God supernaturally provides for people's needs through the generous giving of believers. God graciously promises to meet every need "according to His glorious riches in Christ Jesus" (Philippians 4:19) of those who know how to give sacrificially (vv. 14–18). If we can trust Him for the food that we eat, why can't we trust Him for the building in which we meet?

In the same way that church elders are held to a higher standard of lifestyle and behavior, God's church in corporate form should hold to the highest possible standard of spiritual vision and integrity. Taken to its logical conclusion, the concept of ministry borrowing actually *denies* the reality of God's supernatural provision. How can a ministry leader exhort people to "walk by faith" when he himself has just met with a bank to arrange a loan for a new ministry educational building?

The Dangers of Debt-Free Ministry

Sometimes a ministry can achieve financial freedom but remain in spiritual bondage. That's because finances are not the problem; money woes are simply a sort of "indicator" to reveal the presence of deeper spiritual issues. In fact, a non-borrowing ministry that is spiritually out of balance will experience few real benefits from its financial freedom.

Here are five cautions to beware in your quest to expand your ministry while remaining financially free.

Financial Freedom Can Become a Source of Pride

Don't become judgmental of others who borrow or are in debt. Be sure to guard against both financial and spiritual pride. Ministries, like individuals, can become proud and fall into sin even as they try to obey God. Being debt-free and "borrow-free" can sometimes result in people feeling superior to those who borrow.

Debt-free ministries can sometimes become judgmental and begin to view their financial freedom as a badge of spirituality. Such thinking is completely contrary to God's will. Debt-free ministry should foster intense humility as people realize that God alone has provided the resources to sustain and expand their ministries. How can we be proud of what we did not do? "God opposes the proud but gives grace to the humble" (James 4:6).

Don't allow debt-free ministry to become a source of pride in your life—or in the life of your ministry.

Financial Freedom Can Become an Idol

In some churches, debt-free ministry can become a congregational idol. Debt-free ministries can become too focused on remaining financially free. Although financial freedom is an important aspect of ministry success, it is *not* more important than preaching the gospel or making disciples. Be sure to maintain biblical priorities and recognize that debt-free ministry is only *part* of an overall ministry plan.

Jim recalls one new church that listed "being debt-free" as its foremost doctrinal belief. The pastor was committed to preaching once a month on finances. He constantly exhorted the congregation not to borrow money. Fortunately, in time the pastor realized his imbalance and dealt with it. The church remains debt-free, but it no longer idolizes its financial freedom.

Financial Freedom Can Make a Ministry Overly Cautious

An effort to achieve financial freedom cannot be used as an excuse to become paralyzed with inactivity. Nor should a debt-free ministry philosophy be used to protect the status quo at the cost of reduced effectiveness. The decision to avoid borrowing does not mean that a ministry should stop dreaming or taking healthy risks.

A few years ago a midwestern church was in dire need of additional space. The ministry was challenged by an anonymous donor to start a debt-free building program. The giver proposed that if a $1.5 million building was started before the end of the year, he would match all the funds given up to several hundred thousand dollars. His clear intention was to motivate a congregation he felt was spiritually and financially lethargic.

Some argued against the proposal. They felt the offer was demanding and manipulative. Fortunately, the pastor and the other leaders saw the man's offer as an answer to prayer and a spiritual challenge from God. A vote was taken and the church agreed to raise as much money as possible over a ten-month period.

A contractor was hired and groundbreaking was scheduled. Initially the money came in slowly, and the pastor and other leaders became concerned. Some doubted they had done the right thing. Would the congregation respond? Would the anonymous giver make good on his offer? Would the deadline be met?

After ten months, God once again proved Himself faithful. A spirit of sacrificial giving swept through the church. More than $400,000 was raised. The anonymous giver made good on his offer, and the new building was started two weeks before the original groundbreaking date. It was fully paid for *before* it was finished. And all because the congregation was not afraid to step out on faith and trust God.

Financial Freedom Can Create a False Sense of Ownership

When a ministry finally becomes debt-free, the facilities do *not* belong to those who paid off the loans. But in the case of an east-coast Florida church, paying off the debt raised new problems.

The church's large facility was built during the booming economy of the Apollo space program. And when the Apollo program died in the seventies, the church began to shrink. However, the ministry's large balloon note did not go away, and, eventually, it threatened to bankrupt the church.

The good news is that the congregation persevered and managed to pay off the balloon note. The bad news is that the core group of long-time members who paid off the note then felt as if they owned the church. After all, they reasoned, we paid for it, didn't we? At last report only about a hundred old-time diehards were meeting in a facility designed to serve eight hundred.

In your efforts to remain debt-free, beware of adopting an ownership mentality. Ministry—*like everything else*—belongs only to the sovereign God. We own nothing; we're but stewards, managers for a brief time.

Financial Freedom Can Be Used to Rationalize Materialism

Getting out of debt can sometimes turn into an amassing of riches; wise saving can turn into selfish hoarding. An overemphasis on financial stewardship can cause people to become overly focused on money as a source of security.

Be certain your debt-free ministry also stresses the only truly honorable motive for wanting financial freedom—to increase the glory of God. The parable of the rich fool in Luke 12:16–21 should be a reminder that bigger barns and larger bank accounts are worthless when one stands before God. We are to lay up treasures not on earth, but in heaven (Matthew 6:19–21).

GOD PROVIDES IN OKLAHOMA CITY

When God's people use wise strategies to remain financially free, He honors them with blessings. An inspiring example of how God can bless a ministry when people use the methods suggested in this chapter is the case of a growing church in Oklahoma City.

In the early nineties, a small group of believers led by an energetic young pastor began a new church in the northwest suburbs of Oklahoma City. Determined from the outset to remain financially free, the fledgling church met in homes during the week and in a local high school on Sunday. Within five years, the ministry had grown from thirty to more than five hundred, many of whom were new believers.

As the church grew, the congregation became more and more concerned about the facilities crunch. Feeling a need for their own building, the people began saving money each week toward the purchase of property. Gradually their savings grew to more than $200,000. But the church's planned location was considered a prime real estate area, and land was expensive. The congregation estimated it would take more than $500,000 to buy the ten-to-twenty-acre piece of property it desired.

The temptation was strong to borrow the remainder and buy the land. Instead, church leaders resisted the urge and resolved to take God at His Word that He would enable His people "to abound in every good work" (2 Corinthians 9:8). The people prayed and gave—and waited on the Lord.

Within a few months, a local Christian businessman offered to sell the church a twenty-six-acre tract of land. The location was excellent and included a corner lot with tremendous commercial potential. Best of all, he offered it to the church for only $200,000.

God had once again proved His faithfulness.

At last report, the church had placed the valuable corner lot on the market for $450,000, keeping the rest of the land. When the property sells, that money will fund the largest portion of the church's new metal-building facility —a modest yet functional facility that will be *completely* debt-free.

NOTES

1. Larry Burkett, speech at Fellowship Bible Church, Dalton, Ga., 30 October 1988.
2. John C. LaRue, Jr., "Building, Additions, and Renovation," *Your Church,* November-December, 1994 (accessed via America Online).
3. Ibid.
4. Larry Burkett, *Should Churches Borrow?* (Gainesville, Ga.: Christian Financial Concepts, 1988), 4.
5. Ibid.

6. Ray Bowman with Eddy Hall, *When Not to Build* (Grand Rapids: Baker, 1992), 58.

7. Ibid.

8. Bowman, *When Not to Build,* 58–60.

9. Ibid., 31–32.

CHAPTER 7

DEALING WITH RESISTANCE
Communicating Your Debt-Free Position
While Maintaining Christian Unity

One afternoon, Jim was preparing to leave his office when the phone rang. It was a married couple from Mississippi with questions related to an upcoming vote in their church about borrowing money.

As a volunteer referral counselor and a pastor's seminar instructor for Christian Financial Concepts, Jim regularly gets this kind of call. As with most callers, the couple had waited until the last minute—the church's business meeting was only two days away. And as with most callers, they sounded very sincere—and very concerned.

"Don" was a forty-something, self-employed contractor. He served the church as both a deacon and a Sunday school teacher. His wife "Betty" was also active in several church ministries. Don and Betty had recently attended a CFC financial seminar, during which they became convinced from Scripture that "debt-free living" was what God desired for their family. They were also praying that their church family would reach the same conclusion.

Don and Betty's church had 175 adult members. Their young pastor had been serving the congregation for only two years. He was unsure how to approach the issue of ministry borrowing, but he was earnestly seeking God's will and wanted to do the right thing. The church was less than twenty years old and had borrowed a small amount of money to get started. Until recently, the congregation had been operating under a financial plan that would enable the loan to be completely repaid within five more years.

Then, a few weeks before Don and Betty had called Jim, the owner of a piece of property next to the church had approached the pastor about selling his land to the church. The additional property seemed to be an ideal way to expand their cramped parking and educational facilities, and the congregation was excited about their neighbor's offer to sell.

However, Don and Betty were concerned about the proposal before the church, which was for the church to take out a thirty-year loan to buy the land and build on it. According to the church finance committee, money would be very tight for several years until the church's original loan was paid off. Despite the prospect of five years of touch-and-go finances, the committee had recommended the thirty-year borrowing plan. Don and Betty were concerned that the risk involved was too great for their small church.

Don and Betty reported that they had recently been encouraged after talking with several other couples who shared their desire for the church to be a debt-free ministry. Yet the majority of the congregation seemed to favor borrowing. The discussion that preceded the vote would be pivotal, and Don and Betty wanted to be prepared to properly present their views. Two other deacons, including the chairman, had already told the congregation of their strong opinion that the borrowing plan was the "right thing to do." Don and Betty were hoping and praying that they could persuade the congregation otherwise.

They had three specific questions:

- What could they say in the meeting to encourage the congregation not to borrow?
- How could they best answer the objections of those who believed the church should borrow?
- If the church voted to borrow, should they leave the church—or stay?

Many others across America are asking these same questions, and this chapter is our attempt to provide biblical answers for concerned people. Stay with us, and we'll try to help you find some answers. We'll also tell you how Don and Betty's story ended.

FOR MINISTRY LEADERS:
HOW TO DEAL WITH RESISTANCE

Sometimes the road to non-borrowing ministry is a rocky, rutted, uphill climb. You need practical and useful ideas for communicating your non-borrowing ministry concept. Here are three strategies for ministry leaders to employ when trying to deal effectively and appropriately with congregational or board resistance: praying, modeling, and teaching.

Praying

Prayer is the most powerful means of dealing with the challenges of the Christian life. Pray for your own wisdom, humility, and tenderness as you seek to clearly communicate your convictions. Pray for God to open the minds of His people; to reveal to them His great desire for them to walk by true faith, unaided by the "crutch" of borrowing.

Don't underestimate the often-miraculous power of prayer. But don't forget that you cannot change people; only God can. Change is a process, and it is your responsibility to be *patient*. Allow God whatever time He needs to change people's hearts and minds. And if they never come around to your point of view, continue to love and appreciate them.

Modeling

Demonstrating with your own lifestyle is possibly the most powerful way to communicate truth. Some call teaching by example the "Hebrew educational model" (see Deuteronomy 11:19). The apostle Paul echoed this concept when writing to the Corinthian church (1 Corinthians 4:16: "I urge you to imitate me"). Are you a pastor or ministry leader who wants your ministry to avoid borrowing? Practice what you preach.

We're not suggesting that ministry leaders must pay off the full balance of all their personal loans and mortgages before they can minister. We know from experience that learning to live without borrowing is usually a lengthy process. Yet it is important that church leaders be in the process of becoming financially free. So commit to borrow no more. Otherwise, when you discourage borrowing in your ministry, you'll be like a father who advises his children against smoking while he himself is puffing on a cigar.

Larry Burkett often draws a thought-provoking application out of Luke 16:11. In this verse, Christ poses a serious money-related question to His disciples: "So if you have not been trustworthy in handling worldly wealth, who will trust you with true riches?" Burkett points out that for pastors and ministry leaders this question has foundational implications.

He asks: If pastors and ministry leaders can't handle money wisely, why should people entrust their spiritual lives to them? One of the most basic requirements for spiritual leadership ought to be a financial life that is actively being conformed to the principles of God's Word (1 Timothy 3:3, 8; Titus 1:7).

In addition, be *certain* your entire leadership team agrees with you before you present a non-borrowing concept to your congregation or your supporters. Nothing will short-circuit a non-borrowing movement faster than a lack of unity within leadership.

Teaching

It's the duty of pastors and ministry leaders to teach "the whole will of God" (Acts 20:27). God's will, as revealed in His Word, includes a multitude of clear directives for how His people should manage the resources that He has entrusted to them. It's the job of ministry leaders to teach their people from the Bible. People won't embrace concepts they have seldom (if ever) been taught.

Godly financial instruction can take many forms, including sermons, adult classes, small-group Bible studies, and one-on-one instruction. Materials already exist in abundance if you need them. For more information, refer to the appendix.

Patience is also a key to successful teaching. People need time to come around to a noncultural way of thinking. In our American society—the most materialistic and credit-based in the world—it's difficult to teach concepts (such as living debt-free) that are contrary to what is taught by most schools, colleges, movies, books, and TV programs.

Give people time to digest the idea of forsaking ministry borrowing and depending solely on God's provision. You may also want to share with your people the inspiring success stories of ministries that have forsaken borrowing and debt. Teach from logic, from example, and especially from Scripture. Allow God to work in people's hearts, and trust Him for the outcome.

FOR EVERYONE: RESPONDING TO PRACTICAL ARGUMENTS FOR MINISTRY BORROWING

Some people cite what they consider to be *biblical* justification for a ministry to borrow money. In chapter 4, we presented and dealt with those arguments. In this chapter, we discuss the *pragmatic* arguments people use to justify ministry borrowing (most of which tend to revolve around building). From both a scriptural and a logical perspective, we present and analyze what we have found to be the twelve most common reasons ministries cite for borrowing:

- "Everyone else does it."
- "Borrowing actually saves money, since building costs constantly rise."
- "We're forced to borrow because of urgent ministry needs."
- "Our ministry is too small (or too large)—we don't have enough resources without borrowing."
- "Borrowing is simply how business is done today."
- "If we build it, they will come."
- "Our people will increase their giving to pay off the loan."

- "We can't grow without a permanent facility of our own."
- "Our people will be more motivated to serve in a new facility."
- "Borrowing is the easiest way to expand our ministry."
- "Growing churches are in debt—debt-free churches are dead."
- "It's OK to borrow for appreciating items, like church property."

How many times have you heard these justifications but had no biblical or logical response? We hope the information that follows will help.

"Everyone Else Does It"

It's unfortunate that Christians sometimes try to justify their actions by comparing themselves to the majority. Instead of following popular trends, Christians ought to let biblical principles guide them.

In addition, the argument that "everyone's doing it" is false. As this book points out, many healthy, well-balanced ministries from coast to coast thrive without borrowing.

You'll also find that every biblical reference to borrowing is either a caution or a warning. If "everybody" is indeed "doing it," they are all ignoring God's advice.

There are many healthy, practical, and scriptural alternatives to borrowing (refer to chapters 5 and 6). But if your ministry must borrow, be sure it's for a better reason than "everyone else does it."

"Borrowing Actually Saves Money,
Since Building Costs Constantly Rise"

They say that numbers can be used to prove anything. Some argue that borrowing saves money, since building costs constantly rise. This argument is a good example of how numbers can be manipulated to "prove" almost anything. There are four key points to consider when responding to this line of reasoning:

Point 1: Cheapest is not the best. Purely for the sake of discussion, let's assume for a moment that borrowing actually does save money in the long run. Although Christians must make every effort to be wise stewards of God's resources, the cheapest solution to a problem is often not the best solution. For example, you don't buy church hymnals, pews, and sound systems just because they're the cheapest —you look for quality and value so what you buy with God's money will last. Similarly, you shouldn't be looking for what may seem to be the cheapest way to expand ministry. Rather, you should look for the wisest, the best, and the most effective methods.

Point 2: A "borrow-free" ministry has benefits that transcend mere cost. Let's assume once again that this argument is based on fact. Regardless, we believe that God's best is a total dependence on Him—even if it costs more monetarily. That's because of the tremendous spiritual blessings, benefits, and security that result from a commitment to rely only on God.

Point 3: If you borrow, you'll probably spend more than you need to. When people spend cash, they "feel" it. Letting go of real money has real impact. But when people spend borrowed money, they don't "feel" the spending as deeply. And because the financial impact of spending is softened when people use credit, they generally spend more than they need to. In fact, research by credit-card companies indicates that those who buy with credit cards spend on average about *one-third more* than those who buy with cash.

The same is true for ministries. As Ray Bowman says, "Debt allows us to live beyond our means, to build on our schedule rather than God's."[1] Bowman cites numerous examples of churches that spent beyond their means with borrowed money—and regretted it for years.

Point 4: The argument itself is false. Run the numbers and see for yourself: Borrowing money ultimately costs more whenever interest payments are involved. For example, Bowman says that "depending on how much is borrowed, at what interest rate, and for how long, borrowing

can double or triple the cost of building"[2] when compared
to the cost of building as God provides.

According to Bowman's calculations, a ministry that
builds a $200,000 building and borrows the money for fif-
teen years at 12 percent interest will pay a total of
$432,000. Of that total, $232,000 will be interest (when
calculated in constant dollars).

In contrast, if the ministry were to creatively maximize
its space and save money for a few years, the results would
be entirely different. By setting aside $2,400 each month
(the same amount as payments would be in the borrowing
example) in a building fund earning 10 percent interest, in
only *five years* the ministry would have the $200,000 it
needs to build without borrowing. Then, over the next ten
years, a potential total of $280,000 would be freed up for
ministry (when compared to the overall cost of the borrowing plan). Normal inflation would affect these figures, but
not significantly.

These are not just hypothetical calculations. One pastor
we interviewed shepherded his south Florida church through
a non-borrowing $1.2 million building program in the early
1980s. He told us the ministry had saved *$2.5 million* in
interest by not borrowing, based on the prevailing rates at
that time. At the dedication of the new building, a pastor
from a nearby church stopped by to offer his congratula-
tions. The other pastor's church had just completed a similar
building at a similar cost, but financed over twenty years.
He commented on how alike—yet different—the buildings
were. "Your new facility is paid for," the visiting pastor noted
with a touch of regret, "but we'll be paying on ours for
decades."

Bowman concludes his discussion of interest costs with
this challenge: "While the church must operate within the
world's economic system, it does not have to operate by
the world's principles. When a church follows a financial
plan based solidly on biblical principles, it is largely insu-
lated from the ups and downs of the economy. . . . These
principles are no secret. They have been tried. They work."[3]

"We're Forced to Borrow Because of Urgent Ministry Needs"

This argument can also be stated, "We can't grow without a larger facility, so we need to borrow" or "We've got to have more space to minister effectively, so we need to borrow." The problem with this argument lies in automatically linking the urgent ministry need with a decision to borrow, as if one logically followed the other. They *do not* follow.

Your church may truly need more space. You may be faced with legitimate, pressing ministry opportunities. Your ministry may need a remodeled, different, or additional facility to reach its maximum effectiveness. But borrowing is not the only means to that end; nor is it God's best for His people.

This line of reasoning is most commonly used when making a case for building. With that fact in mind, consider these four points when responding to the borrow-because-of-urgency argument:

Point 1: New facilities may not be God's will for your church right now. The tension your ministry is experiencing as a result of needs that seem urgent may be God trying to get your people's attention. God may be trying to redirect your ministry into a new type of service. If your church has reached a certain size, the Lord may be moving your congregation to multiply itself and establish a daughter church in a more needy part of your community. God may be seeking to deepen your church's walk with Him. Or He may want to bring revival and recommitment, in preparation for upcoming challenges.

For example, consider the situation of Fellowship Bible Church in 1991. Approaching the church's twentieth anniversary, many sensed that the ministry was lacking vitality and direction. For several years there had been talk of building a new facility. Some suggested a new building would be the answer to the church's problems. The building project, they reasoned, would excite and unite the people. Some felt the church should borrow and immediately begin building.

Most people, however, wanted to remain true to Fellowship's non-borrowing commitment. The elders decided to wait, pray, and seek God for another solution.

In retrospect, many believe the decision to seek God rather than build was a pivotal decision in the church's history. After continuing prayer and discussion, Fellowship's elders concluded that the solution to the church's "problem" did not lie in physical programs, but in spiritual revival. So the elders invited Al Whittinghill of Ambassadors for Christ (an Atlanta-based church renewal ministry) to lead the church in a week-long "Spiritual Life Conference."

The entire congregation fasted and prayed in preparation for the conference. And God did not fail; He met the church's need in a glorious outpouring of Spirit-led revival and renewal.

Even today, Fellowship members are experiencing the benefits of their 1991 revival. As God's Spirit moved powerfully during the conference, God's people cried out in repentance and recommitment, kneeling at the altar, in the aisles, and throughout the sanctuary. In addition to the changed and renewed lives of church members, the revival began to spread into the community as the congregation began talking with friends and loved ones about what God had done.

Jim later said, "I'm confident that if we had decided to go ahead with the building instead of waiting and seeking God's direction, we would have missed a tremendous blessing. Sometimes a building program can distract people from what God is trying to do among them."

Don't assume that God is automatically saying "Build!" when seemingly urgent ministry needs appear. First look for what He may be trying to accomplish in people's lives.

But if your ministry feels it needs to borrow, first take Ray Bowman's "Need Test" (*When Not to Build*, p. 79) and "Finance Test" (p. 107). If you take these "tests" honestly, your ministry may reconsider its intention to build.

Point 2: There are many ways to grow without borrowing. Borrowing should be a ministry's last alternative rather than its first choice. You have a wide range of biblical and practical options—explore them all with open minds *before* your ministry decides to borrow. We won't belabor this point; it's covered well in chapters 5 and 6.

Point 3: God may be leading you to minister outside your traditional facility. In today's fragmented and multi-faceted culture, not everyone can be reached and discipled through conventional American church buildings. Rather than building a larger facility to bring people in, perhaps God is leading your ministry to turn its attention outward. Remember that most of the world does not—and will never —look to the church for wisdom. That's why Jesus commands us to do what He did: "*go* and make disciples . . ." (Matthew 28:19, italics added).

We're not saying that every local church must set up an inner-city ministry; there may not even be an "inner city" in your town. However, we are saying that the Savior *expects* every ministry to have a healthy outreach in its local community *and* into the world.

Outreach is seldom accomplished by buildings. Pray earnestly about how God might have your ministry "move out" instead of "build up."

Point 4: Facilities do not equal ministry. For about the first four hundred years of its existence, the church was virtually without buildings of its own. Yet during those four centuries, the church of Jesus Christ swept like a tidal wave across the known world. Millions placed their faith in Christ. Gathering in homes, businesses, city squares, public theaters, and country fields, they transformed the world for eternity. And with *no buildings*.

It's dangerous to equate facilities with ministry—that way of thinking is a symptom of a "fortress" mentality. If Christians needed buildings to effectively minister, the growth of the early church would have been impossible. In fact, if buildings were *needed* for ministry, most of God's work that is currently taking place in the Third World would be impossible. God commands believers to be ministers and ambassadors, not builders.

We're not saying ministries shouldn't construct effective and appropriate facilities as God provides the resources. But *ministry* can, does, and *must* take place anywhere and everywhere. Buildings are, and always have been, optional.

"Our Ministry Is Too Small (or Too Large)—
We Don't Have Enough Resources Without Borrowing"

When any faithful ministry—whether small or large—
trusts God to provide, He will do so abundantly. But He
provides as He sees fit, and often in ways that confound
and amaze. If He wants your small (or large) ministry to
expand into new areas, He'll provide the funds.

Here are three points to think and pray about as you
consider expanding your ministry:

**Point 1: God's best is never thwarted by an apparent
lack of funds.** In fact, God sometimes uses an apparent
lack of funds to test our ability to trust Him. As we have
already stated, many Christian organizations (small and
large) fall into the materialistic trap of equating facilities
with ministry. God, who graciously provides everything
His people need, is not bound by human constraints of urgency or size.

We have discovered a wonderful principle regarding the
"we-don't-have-the-resources" argument for borrowing.
Simply stated, the principle is this: *Yes, you do!* You *do*
have the resources you need! God has sovereignly placed
those resources under the stewardship of your people. You
may not always have all the resources you *want,* but
wouldn't you rather let God decide whether or not you
need something that you want?

The question is: How willing are your people to *give* generously and sacrificially? Whether it's in the form of unneeded land, heirlooms, jewelry, surplus retirement funds,
extra clothing, automobiles, or whatever, if expansion is
indeed necessary God has placed the resources you need
for it within the control of the people who support your
ministry. Other resources God has given your people may
include such valuable things as creative thinking, flexibility, or even construction skills. Don't discount anything of
value.

So please accept this challenge in the spirit of love that
we intend it: *If your people are not spiritually mature
enough to give generously and sacrificially, your ministry
may not yet be ready for expansion.* But when people learn

how to give sacrificially, churches and other ministries will learn first-hand about God's best means of provision and will never lack for resources.

Point 2: Even a small number of God's people can accomplish great things. Especially for those in smaller ministries, it's vital to remember that God is not hampered by human limitations of urgency or size. Throughout time, He has accomplished amazing things with only a few people. But those people were willing to act outside of their own understanding. They were prepared to trust God when they couldn't see the way. And they were so familiar with the character of God that they believed He would abundantly provide for them.

Consider the example of Gideon (Judges 6:1–8:32). When God chose Gideon to free the impoverished nation of Israel from the oppression of the Midianites, the Lord commanded him to "go in *the strength you have* and save Israel . . ." (Judges 6:14, italics added). Not finding this especially reassuring, Gideon replied, "How can I save Israel? My clan is the weakest . . . and I am the least in my family" (v. 15). God's answer should ring to us down through the ages, encouraging us whenever we feel overpowered by life's challenges: *"I will be with you . . ."* (v. 16, italics added).

Point 3: Let God "grow" you into ministry before you "go" into ministry. Regardless of your ministry's size, if you expand only within the means that God provides, you'll never be in a position of "getting ahead" of God. We're not saying that your ministry should do nothing and adopt a "let-go-and-let-God" apathy when it comes to expansion and growth. Rather, we're encouraging you to be patient. Let God work in the hearts of His people. Then grow only as Christ's own body works together to fund that growth.

Also, be careful not to fall into the trap of thinking, "We'll trust God for the growth we need to pay back our loan." That's not trusting God; that's presuming on the future. We've already explained *from Scripture* that trusting God to sovereignly provide is God's best for His church.

God is under no obligation to bail us out when we con-
sciously choose something other than His best.

"Borrowing Is Simply How Business Is Done Today"

The response to this line of reasoning ought to be obvious—just because something is "business as usual" does
not automatically make it applicable to Christian ministry.
Although it's true that borrowing has become pandemic in
our society, God's ways are rarely those of the world.

Some say, "Borrowing is just another modern method.
How can it be any more wrong than electric lights or air-
conditioning?" The answer is two-fold: *First,* borrowing—
in all its complexities—is as ancient as man himself; there's
nothing "new" about it. *Second,* it's invalid to compare
borrowing to technological advancements. For example,
God never warned anyone in the Bible about the dangers of
electric lights. However, God's Word is replete with em-
phatic cautions against borrowing.

What we're urging is the adoption of a truly biblical model
for ministry financing. Consider this story from Larry
Burkett:

> I had a pastor friend who was asked to speak at a Rotary
> Club meeting. During his speech, he gave a testimony about
> the large new facility his church was building in that commu-
> nity. He said, "I want to tell you about the miracle God has
> done for our church—we are building our new facility with a 6
> percent loan from the best bank in town. And we got the loan
> without even having adequate collateral! It's a real miracle
> from God!"
>
> At that moment, a member of the club who was sitting in
> the back of the room stood up. He said, "Pastor, I built my
> liquor business the same way. I didn't know God was even in
> the liquor business!"
>
> The owner of the liquor business was not impressed with
> what the pastor had to say. That's because God could get no
> glory for the church getting a loan. That pastor had no spiritual
> message to deliver, only one that was completely human.
>
> I don't know that an unbeliever would see it as an absolutely
> miraculous testimony of God, but I guarantee this: If you build
> a church debt-free, you will impress him.[4]

"If We Build It, They Will Come"

Beware of this "field-of-dreams" mind-set. "Build and they will come" is *not* a scriptural concept. If your ministry is not growing now, God will not fill up a bigger building simply because it's there. Neither will He bring in resources to support a new, expensive program that He Himself didn't begin. Consider these two important points:

Borrowing to expand ministry runs the risk of later stagnation. Because borrowing to expand ministry ignores scriptural models, the benefits of true unity and harmony often do not result. Borrowing reduces people's personal involvement in the process of expansion. As a result, they do not feel as deeply and as intimately connected to the ministry as they would if the expansion were the direct result of their own sacrificial commitment. As Bowman has pointed out, many ministries that borrow to expand end up stagnating during the loan payback period.

Beware of those who seek ministries with impressive facilities. It's nice to have attractive facilities. But a modest, maximized, well-maintained facility that has a real impact in its community is more valuable to God than a state-of-the-art MegaWorshipCenter where a crowd of spectators comes to be entertained and impressed. We're not saying that every large, impressive church is made up of only shallow Christians. We are saying that constant focus on the appearance of facilities increases the likelihood of attracting spectators.

We're not condemning the megachurch. Every ministry has its advantages and disadvantages. But small ministries have much to offer and nothing to be ashamed of regarding their size. God builds His church, and He builds ministries in all sizes. But in a modest ministry it's much more difficult to be a spectator than it is in a larger one.

"Our People Will Increase Their Giving to Pay Off the Loan"

This argument might also be stated, "If we borrow, they will give." Initially, this reasoning might even be true. The excitement of a building going up, or a new area of ministry starting, often elicits an enthusiastic and generous first response. But this argument indicates a fundamental mis-understanding of the nature of Christian generosity.

The Bible clearly states that generous giving is not the result of external influences, but of *intrinsic* motivation. People give generously and consistently because their core belief system *demands* that they do so. According to Scripture, generous givers are those who have "[given] themselves first to the Lord" (2 Corinthians 8:5).

Generous giving is a "litmus test" that verifies the presence of love for God in a person's heart. Paul says of his instructions to the Corinthians for giving to the support of his ministry: "I am not commanding you, but I want to *test the sincerity of your love*" (2 Corinthians 8:8, italics added).

People may initially be excited about giving to support a project that involves borrowing. However, the initial excitement always wanes. All too soon, the ministry shifts its focus and the former hot project becomes just another loan to pay off. And church fund-raisers have told us that loan payoff serves as perhaps the *weakest* of all motivations for people to give.

Unless your people are enthusiastically demonstrating sincere love for Christ by their current levels of generous giving, there is little reason to assume they will rise to the occasion in support of paying off a loan. And consider this: If your ministry is already supported by committed and sincere givers, you probably won't have much need to borrow in the first place.

"We Can't Grow Without a Permanent Facility of Our Own"

Sometimes people believe that others won't take a ministry seriously unless it's located at a "permanent" site. If your ministry is made up of committed disciples, a temporary site will erect no barriers to meeting people's needs, building up the body of Christ, or evangelizing the world. In ministry, it's attitude, motivation, and the power of God's Holy Spirit that make the difference. Facilities—permanent or otherwise—matter little.

On the other hand, if your ministry is not made up of committed disciples, you've got a much more serious problem on your hands. We recommend spiritual growth before you even *begin* to think about permanent facilities.

"Our People Will Be More Motivated to Serve in a New Facility"

This argument is often put forward when a loan is being used to construct new facilities or remodel existing ones. However, this line of reasoning reflects a misunderstanding of the nature of Christian service.

The Bible makes clear that selfless service, like giving, is the result of intrinsic motivation. Some people are motivated by obligation, duty, pride, or fear. Those people are a part of every ministry. But they are usually not the ones who make up the ministry's core group of volunteers.

According to Jesus, the only enduring source of real motivation has nothing to do with the age of a ministry's facilities. He said, "If you love me, you will obey what I command" (John 14:15). *Service* is the core concept of the Christian lifestyle. Jesus said even He Himself "did not come to be served, but to serve" (Matthew 20:28).

The people who make up the core of your ministry's committed volunteers give of their time and energy because they love God, not because they love a building or a program. If your people aren't serving in your current ministry environment, you can't reasonably expect them to serve in a new one. In fact, just the opposite often happens —people become complacent and comfortable after the new building is finished or the newest program is completed.

"Borrowing Is the Easiest Way to Expand Our Ministry"

Yes, we acknowledge that borrowing is easy. That's what makes it so alluring. But there's nothing in Scripture to indicate that an easy alternative justifies a lack of trust in God. In fact, throughout God's Word His people have lived their most fulfilled lives when faced by adversity and challenge. As Paul said to the Corinthian church about his planned trip to visit them: "A great door for effective work has opened to me, and there are many who oppose me" (1 Corinthians 16:9). Paul understood that opposition to doing God's work in God's way is a sure sign that His people are on the right track.

If people won't sacrifice their material resources, what will they sacrifice? God's work ought to be funded by the generous gifts of God's people. Giving, according to the apostle Paul, is a visible, outward indicator of the inner condition of a Christian's relationship with God. Consider what Paul said about giving in his second letter to the Corinthians: He told them to pattern themselves after the Macedonians (i.e., the Philippians), who "gave even beyond their ability" (2 Corinthians 8:3).

Remember Paul's "litmus test" in verses 7 and 8? Paul is saying, "Go ahead—prove your love for Christ by your sacrificial giving." This is exactly how the church must be challenged. Our experience in years of counseling hundreds of families has demonstrated to us over and over that until Christians open their wallets and purses to God, their commitment to Him remains at a very basic level. A life of true discipleship is virtually impossible for the Christian whose pocketbook is not actively surrendered to God. Although it is perhaps the most rewarding aspect of ministry, sacrificial giving is never the easiest way to expand ministry.

"Growing Churches Are in Debt—Debt-Free Churches Are Dead"

Some go so far as to say, "We'll stop growing if we don't borrow." This line of reasoning is nothing more than self-deception. It's God's Spirit that gives life to a ministry—*not* an infusion of cash. "Dead" ministries are dead whether they borrow or not. If your ministry is truly dying, borrowing (by itself) is not even an effective treatment, much less a cure. A loan may only prolong a dying ministry's agony and make its ultimate demise even more painful.

Remember that dying ministries can be large or small, rural or urban, completely debt-free or heavily leveraged. Is God's Holy Spirit conforming your people to the image of Christ? If not, you have serious problems you need to deal with regardless of how you fund your ministry.

It's *faith* that makes the church come alive, not loans. And most of the non-borrowing churches we interviewed were vibrantly alive in the Spirit. God wants His people to trust Him and His sovereign provision, rather than relaxing in the apparent security of worldly borrowing plans. He commands us to "live by faith" (Habakkuk 2:4; Hebrews 10:38). And what is faith? "Faith is being sure of what we hope for and *certain of what we do not see*" (Hebrews 11:1, italics added). A loan delivers the instant gratification our culture hungers for, but it takes *true* faith to wait on God.

"It's OK to Borrow for Appreciating Items, Like Church Property"

The issue at stake in ministry borrowing is not a question of "OK" or "not OK." Practically, it's a question of risk and wisdom. Spiritually, it's a question of conforming to biblical principles and ministry models and following God's individual guidance. As we've said repeatedly in this book, it's not a sin to borrow.

Ministries borrow for a variety of reasons, many of which do not involve land or property. We agree that when real estate is involved, possible appreciation is an important consideration. But ministry properties do not always appreciate.

We checked with several bank loan officers about the value of ministry property. They agreed that church property is usually difficult to sell and often is sold at a loss. This is primarily due to the specialized nature of how churches develop property. When a church sells property, the sale is often to a commercial business. And commercial businesses almost always remodel, renovate, or destroy and rebuild.

One church in central Florida purchased ten acres of land in 1988 for $700,000. The congregation hoped to build a new building to replace their existing facility, but the plans were never finalized. Some began to speak of selling the ten-acre property and refocusing on more efficient development of their existing building. When the *same property* was appraised in 1995 by the *same appraiser,* it was valued at only $250,000!

It's important to note that none of the arguments in this chapter are biblical in nature. Rather, the contentions we've just examined are *pragmatic.* We seldom have to deal with attempts to support ministry borrowing from a biblical basis (but for those arguments, refer to chapter 4).

FOR THE CONGREGATION: PERSUADING LEADERSHIP TO EMBRACE "BORROW-FREE" MINISTRY

Remember that change in a church is often like turning an ocean liner—it's a slow and deliberate process that takes a lot of time and horsepower. God is the One who changes hearts—according to His own timing. So in your zeal to share your opinion, be certain you don't get involved in a battle with your ministry leaders.

Let's look at five biblical and practical strategies that people can use to persuade their ministry leaders to get out of debt and eliminate or minimize borrowing: pray, model, approach, present, and teach information.

Pray

Pray consistently and fervently, not only for your ministry leaders but for yourself. Prayer may be especially important if your leaders are resistant or reluctant. God changes hearts when the most eloquent of arguments cannot.

Model

It's important that your own personal finances are under the Spirit's direction. Try to "practice what you preach" as much as possible. To the best of your ability, live a life of godly financial principles, such as those presented in chapter 9.

Approach

Be sure to approach your leaders with honor and respect. Your first contact when trying to address the issue of ministry borrowing ought to be the ministry leader or leaders. *Don't* start a damaging and divisive grass-roots gossip campaign. *Do* deal directly with the ministry or church authorities who can initiate and lead a change. We recommend that you give your leaders:

- *Good information.* We highly recommend *When Not to Build* by Ray Bowman and Eddy Hall. For an in-depth look at personal debt and borrowing, we also recommend *Debt-Free Living* or *Investing for the Future* by Larry Burkett and *Money, Possessions, and Eternity* by Randy Alcorn.

- *Time.* Be patient as your ministry leaders assimilate the information you supply. They will most likely not be persuaded overnight. If possible, don't wait until the last minute before the church votes to borrow—start giving your leaders debt-free and "borrow-free" information even *before* a specific borrowing issue comes up.

Present

Request an opportunity to make a respectful presentation to the entire leadership team. If your offer is accepted, be well-prepared, tactful, tasteful, thorough, and biblical. If your ministry's borrowing decisions are made at the denominational level, be sure to contact the proper denominational authorities to present your case.

Teach

Get permission to teach biblical financial principles in your church or ministry. For example, you might lead a CFC "How to Manage Your Money" Bible study. Or you could get your church involved in the Crown Ministries small-group Bible study. Change often comes slowly to Christian ministries, especially churches. Sometimes long-term change from the "bottom up" is the only way to address the problems of church borrowing or debt.

You may not be able to affect the immediate borrowing issue that concerns you, or even the next one, but eventually sound biblical teaching on borrowing and debt will alter the climate of your ministry. As more and more people learn what the Bible says about personal borrowing and debt, they will be more likely to avoid borrowing and debt in corporate ministry.

PRESERVING UNITY

In Ephesians 4:3, Paul commands us to "Make every effort to keep the unity of the Spirit through the bond of peace." This is but one of the Bible's many calls for unity among God's people. Although the issue of church borrowing is often inflammatory, it's not a concept over which Christians ought to divide. We've made a strong case in this book against borrowing, but we're not willing to go to war with other believers over the issue.

Christian unity and harmony are essential elements of a healthy ministry. With that in mind, we've identified four important cautions that believers should carefully consider in order to preserve unity while dealing with church borrowing and debt issues:

- Move slowly.
- Share your convictions properly.
- If all else fails, compromise.
- Honor and obey your ministry leaders.

Paying proper attention to each of these cautions will help you do everything you can to preserve unity and avoid borrowing-related divisiveness.

Move Slowly

Borrowing is a way of life for most of our culture, and it's a philosophy—a *lifestyle*—that often cannot be easily or quickly set aside. As Lewis Abbott and others point out, borrowing to expand ministry has also become the normal, accepted practice of Christians.

Be patient. Don't try to artificially accelerate the development of a non-borrowing conviction in your church. Give people time to change their minds, as you pray for them and reason with them. Don't lose sight of the fact that it's not a sin to borrow (in and of itself)—even though it is risky. Borrowed money is not worth dividing the church.

Share Your Convictions Properly

You can't force a non-borrowing conviction on your fellow believers, so don't try. When you explain your beliefs, do so in a loving and kind manner. But before you tell others of your convictions, ask yourself these three questions:

Question 1: Is this a good time? Be sure it's a good time to share your thoughts. For example, a moment of high tension during an emotion-packed church budget meeting may not be the ideal time to present a passionate argument against borrowing. Then again, for your ministry, it might be the perfect time. Just be sensitive to the people around you. And men—be sure to trust your wives if they advise you not to speak!

Question 2: Is this a good place? It may be much more persuasive for you to share your convictions in a private setting rather than in public. For example, a series of one-on-one breakfast meetings with individual members of the building committee may be much more effective than a ten-against-one confrontation.

Question 3: Is this the right person? If you need to persuade anyone, it's your ministry leaders. In most cases, people will follow their leaders—so try to tactfully and respectfully persuade your leaders first.

Don't be afraid to approach your ministry leaders with the concept of "borrow-free" ministry. If they are the mature, godly people that Scripture requires them to be—and if you approach them properly—they will welcome (or at least permit) an open and fair discussion of the concept.

If All Else Fails, Compromise

Perhaps you've diligently and prayerfully examined all your alternatives. After much discussion and debate, you've determined that your ministry most likely cannot or will not avoid borrowing now. If current borrowing seems unavoidable, suggest compromises, such as:

- Adopting a policy of no additional borrowing in the future
- Borrowing only a small amount, for a short term
- Using a no-interest bond issue or similar plan that eliminates surety

Even those who advocate borrowing are usually against "excessive" borrowing—what they often call "excessive

debt." So if you feel your ministry simply *must* borrow, try to
secure a loan that is as small and as short-term as possible.
For more details on biblical borrowing, refer to chapter 8.

Honor and Obey Your Ministry Leaders

Don't be rebellious or contentious. The issue of borrowing money, while important, is not worth a church split or
a mass exodus from the ministry.

In your efforts to help your ministry avoid borrowing
money, remember that believers are clearly commanded to
obey those in leadership. Obedience to church leaders is
almost unheard of in the modern, individualistic American
church, but such obedience is still God's command. Hebrews 13:17 clearly says, "Obey your leaders and submit to
their authority. They keep watch over you as men who
must give an account. Obey them so that their work will be
a joy, not a burden."

You may be thinking about disassociating yourself from
a ministry or leaving a church that has decided to borrow
money. However, unless a ministry is involved in actual
wrongdoing, we advise against that course of action. Our
counsel: Remain. Submit to your leaders. Don't be divisive
or contentious. Instead, be encouraging and affirming. The
ministry that borrows may someday come to believe that
borrowing has deprived them of God's highest blessings. It
may then need your help.

THE CONCLUSION OF DON AND BETTY'S STORY

Remember the story of Don and Betty? We're pleased to
report that their situation had a favorable outcome. After
praying with them and telling them much of the information in this chapter, Jim arranged to speak with their pastor by phone.

The pastor called Jim the morning before the business
meeting. As Don and Betty had said, he was sincerely seeking God's direction. He had given a great deal of thought to
the issue of ministry borrowing, and he asked penetrating
questions. Yet as Jim hung up the phone after their forty-
five minute conversation, he was unsure what the pastor
would actually recommend to his church.

Three weeks later Don and Betty called back with real excitement in their voices. The seller of the property had agreed to lease his land to the church for five years, after which the church would have a lease/purchase option that allowed the congregation to pay cash for the property. At the business meeting, the pastor had explained why he felt that borrowing was not God's way. He gave his opinion that the new building should wait until the church had paid off its existing loan.

It turned out that many in the congregation felt the same way, but they were simply waiting for their pastor to lead them in that direction. Of course, several members didn't agree with the pastor's new-found convictions, including the two aforementioned deacons. So Don and Betty prayerfully and respectfully invited the deacons and their wives, along with any other interested members, to attend a six-week Bible study in their home. The topic: "What the Bible Says About Money."

As they ended their conversation with Jim, Don and Betty were thankful and elated. They had seen God work in their pastor and in their fellow church members.

Don and Betty are good examples of the best way to deal with resistance to the concept of non-borrowing ministry. They were committed, informed, and prepared to discuss the issues. But they were also tactful, respectful, humble, and submissive to those in ministering authority. They handled themselves well, and God blessed their efforts.

NOTES

1. Ray Bowman with Eddy Hall, *When Not to Build* (Grand Rapids: Baker, 1992), 87.
2. Ibid., 90.
3. Ibid., 90–91.
4. Larry Burkett, speech at Fellowship Bible Church, Dalton, Ga., 17 May 1992.

CHAPTER 8

LENDING AND BORROWING WITHIN THE CHURCH
Lending and Borrowing with Wisdom—Exploring Biblical Guidelines

Because you've stayed with us this far, we assume that you're at least moderately interested in the concept of non-borrowing ministry. You may even be convinced that non-borrowing ministry is the best way to go. And if you've been trying to get your church to minister without borrowing, you may have already tried much of what we've suggested.

"But," you say, "I've tried everything, and nothing has worked. The church still plans to borrow money. What can I do now?"

Good question. We have some answers and several options for you to explore. Let's look at the subject of biblical borrowing.

"Biblical borrowing?" you may ask. "Doesn't that concept run contrary to everything you've been saying?"

Another good question. Read on and learn the answer.

SCRIPTURAL BORROWING GUIDELINES

In case you haven't got the message by now, we'll say it again, as plainly as possible: It's not a sin to borrow, but it *is* unnecessarily risky. Borrowing is mentioned repeatedly in Scripture, but almost always as a caution—or, in the form of debt, as a curse. Randy Alcorn notes that "Scripture speaks of debt [and borrowing] with the utmost sobriety. Debt is warned against throughout Proverbs, God's book of practical wisdom. . . . Debt is described as bondage. . . . Scripture definitely discourages debt."[1]

Scripture takes a negative view of the concepts of borrowing and debt. (For a sample listing of Scriptures, refer to the list of passages on page 28.) That's a primary reason that any Bible-based ministry should avoid borrowing. However, if your ministry feels it cannot avoid borrowing, these five guidelines may prove helpful:

- Borrow only as a last resort.
- Take out only short-term or low-interest loans.
- Borrow only from Christians.
- Never become surety for a loan.
- Always repay—on time, and in full.

Borrow Only as a Last Resort

We believe that *a ministry should borrow money only as a last resort.* God's highest preference for His people is to operate without borrowing. The repeated scriptural model for funding ministry is not borrowing. It's giving. God has promised to meet all the needs of the church. But He wants to do it through joyous, generous, and sacrificial giving of His people.

Despite our exhortation, we realize that many ministries will continue to borrow money regardless. Larry Burkett suggests, "A reasonable compromise is to borrow from God's people through bonds or by some other means. At least then God's people supply and receive His money."[2]

If your church or ministry does borrow money, for building or any other reason, do it with your eyes wide open! Note that you can borrow without getting into debt (i.e., being unable to repay). But debt almost always is the result of excessive borrowing. So don't ignore the many cautions of Scripture. Acknowledge the risk you're taking, borrow with great care, and minimize the term of the loan.

Another word of caution: In your zeal to avoid borrowing in your ministry, be sure not to emulate the odd practices of some churches. A case in point is a church that Ron Blue once attended. He remembers that "we were encouraged to go out and borrow money to give to the church. The church wanted to be debt-free—but we [the congregation] wouldn't be!"[3]

Take Out Only Short-Term or Low-Interest Loans

Although the church is under no specific "law" in the age of grace, scriptural models clearly teach that borrowing should be for only a short time. The Old Testament biblical limit was seven years (Deuteronomy 15:1; Nehemiah 10:31). Generally speaking, the shorter the term of a loan, the less the risk. And as we have previously noted, even those who recommend ministry borrowing agree that what they call "excessive" interest should always be avoided.

Scriptural principles prohibit the concept of interest payments among God's people. The benefit? When you don't pay interest, you can put the money into ministry instead.

For ministries that simply must borrow, we recommend *only* no-interest loans and bond issues. This is based on the model that God's people are not to demand *any* interest (usury) from each other (Exodus 22:25; Leviticus 25:37; Nehemiah 5:10–13).

Borrow Only from Christians

Remember that the church is under no borrowing-related "laws." However, we have powerful *examples* in Scripture. God challenged the Israelites that if they fully obeyed Him, carefully followed all His commandments, and did not follow or serve other gods, His people would "lend to many nations but [would] borrow from none" (Deuteronomy 28:12).

Even in New Testament times, the apostle John commended a group of traveling preachers to his friend Gaius for financial aid, in large part because those "brothers" refused financial help "from the pagans" (3 John 5–8).

Again, scriptural principles are clear: The church is to turn to its own—not to the world—for financial help.

Never Become Surety for a Loan

Remember our definition of surety from chapter 1? Briefly stated, it means "agreeing to be responsible for paying off someone else's financial obligations" or "pledging more than you have as security for another's obligations." Example: co-signing for a loan even if you know you can't pay if the other person defaults.

You may also recall that Solomon denounced surety in the book of Proverbs. Among other cautions, the Bible says those who stand surety "will surely suffer" (11:15). They are also "lacking in judgment" (17:18). For further understanding, we recommend a study of Proverbs 6:1–5; 20:16; and 22:26–27.

"So what's your point?" you may be asking. Simply this: If you are a church or ministry leader who signs the papers for your ministry's loan, the loan ought to be fully collateralized. Either that, or you must be able to pay the entire amount *yourself* if the ministry cannot. And don't forget that whether you can or can't pay, you're still in surety just by *guaranteeing the loan!*

More and more, creditors are holding the signers of ministry notes personally responsible for the balance of the loan if the ministry defaults. Unfortunately, many families have been financially ruined in this way.

Even without the threat of personal financial ruin, Christians should strongly resist the temptation to do what God counsels *not* to do. So be sure any loans to your ministry are fully collateralized, with resources both you and your ministry can afford to lose. Don't let your ministry get involved in surety. And if you're in surety, take Solomon's advice. Do whatever it takes to get out.

Always Repay—on Time, and in Full

"The wicked borrow and do not repay" is the biblical principle from Psalm 37:21 that governs the repayment of borrowed resources. There is no equivocation here—only those who are wicked (evil, sinful) fail to repay what they have borrowed. Romans 13:8 also commands, "Let no debt remain outstanding [i.e., unpaid]."

Why is repayment so important? Because the testimony and glory of Jesus Christ are at stake. Christians must not let the name of Christ be ridiculed as a result of ministries failing to pay what they owe. Consider the tower-building example Jesus used to illustrate the cost of discipleship (Luke 14:28–30). As with all parables, this story is meaningful at two levels: the physical example used and the spiritual message intended. Because borrowing is risky, count the cost of full, on-time repayment.

Be sure the money you borrow can be repaid *even in a worst-case scenario*. Don't put God's ministry at unnecessary risk. Don't allow your ministry—and Christ's name—to be ridiculed when you cannot complete the job. With borrowed money, the project isn't finished until the loan is paid in full.

PROBLEMS WITH BONDS

When a church finances expansion with a bond issue, the ministry is essentially borrowing from itself. Here's how it works: Church members (and possibly other investors) purchase the bonds, thus lending their money to the ministry for the term of the bonds. When the bonds mature after a period of time, the ministry pays back those who purchased them, usually with interest. In this way, money is more likely to "stay within" the ministry.

Some bond issues appear to succeed. Bonds are sold, ministry expands, and the bonds are repaid with no obvious problems. However, bonds can be virtual time-bombs, just waiting to explode. Consider these four potential problems:

- Charging Christians interest violates biblical principles.
- Bonds presume on the future.
- Bonds contradict biblical giving imperatives.
- Bonds can intensify other ministry problems.

Charging Christians Interest Violates Biblical Principles

Historically, and according to Scripture, interest and usury are the same thing.

The scriptural principle is clear: While God's people are permitted to charge interest to unbelievers, they are *not* to charge interest (usury) of *any amount* to their fellow believers. Consider these passages:

- Exodus 22:25—"If you lend money to one of my people among you who is needy, do not be like a moneylender; charge him no interest."

- Leviticus 25:35–37—"If one of your countrymen becomes poor and is unable to support himself . . . do not take interest of any kind from him, but fear your God, so that your countryman may continue to live among you. You must not lend him money at interest or sell him food at a profit."

- Deuteronomy 23:19–20—"Do not charge your brother interest, whether on money or food or anything else that may earn interest. You may charge a foreigner interest, but not a brother Israelite, so that the Lord your God may bless you in everything you put your hand to in the land you are entering to possess."

Interest (usury) was widely practiced in the ancient world. Rates in some places (such as northern Assyria in the fifteenth century B.C.) were as high as *50 percent.*[4] However, God has always called His people to be different from other nations. He wants them to live by a higher standard—His own example of compassion and kindness.

That's the point God makes in Leviticus 25:38. After commanding Israel not to charge any interest, He explains, "I am the Lord your God, who brought you out of Egypt to give you the land of Canaan and to be your God." Just as God graciously brought them out of Egypt and *gave* them the land, so the Israelites were to be gracious and give to one another. They were to count their relationships with each other as more important than financial gain.

God promised the Israelites that if they lived by His "no-interest" lending plan, He would "bless" everything they did in the Promised Land. Today, God is waiting to bless individual Christians and ministries that put compassion ahead of profit and generosity ahead of greed.

Bonds Presume on the Future

All too often, church bond issues are based on potentially unsound assumptions of what the future may hold. Some of these assumptions include:

- The ministry will grow as a result of the expanded facilities.
- The financial base will grow enough for the bonds to be repaid.
- There will not be a church split, pastoral change, or other church-shrinking crisis while the bonds are maturing.
- There will not be an economic downturn while the bonds are maturing.
- God does not have other uses for the ministry's future surplus funds, such as disaster relief, spreading the gospel message to unreached people, or responding to unforeseen ministry emergencies.

It's dangerous to presume upon the future. James 4:13–16 equates presumption with arrogance and tells us that "all such boasting is evil" (v. 16). We're *not* saying that ministries should never step out and move by faith. We *are* saying that they should be careful to distinguish between the leading of God and human presumption. God's method calls for taking freewill offerings and then proceeding when enough is collected; the human method is to borrow now and pay back later.

Church management consultant David Pollock has some interesting comments on the subject of church bonds. Once while Pollock was a guest on Larry Burkett's *Money Matters* radio program, a caller told the story of a church in the Northeast that defaulted on its bonds when the pas-

tor was found with his hand in the fund. The church folded
and its assets were liquidated. However, the money raised
was insufficient to pay off the church's indebtedness. As a
result, the lender (a bank) charged each member between
$5,000 and $7,000 to make up the difference! The caller
told of another church in his area that was offering bonds
at an attractive interest rate, and he wanted Pollock's opinion on church bonds. Pollock replied, "Isn't it interesting
that a church which can't qualify [for a bank loan] will
qualify with certain bonding companies? Bonds are just
another way of borrowing [and] the people of a church can
become liable for the proceeds of that bond if they default.
Read the fine print. Because the church [often is registered
as] a corporation, and they vote, the court could easily say
[that the] people voted as members. That's why I don't like
bond programs."[5]

Bonds Contradict Biblical Giving Imperatives

Jesus Himself said that we are to "lend" without expecting anything back (Luke 6:34–35). God repeatedly praises
those who "lend freely," expecting nothing in return
(Psalm 37:26; 112:5; Proverbs 19:17). We must not ignore
the many biblical examples of God's sovereign funding of
His ministry efforts throughout the ages.

Bonds Can Intensify Other Ministry Problems

Bonds indicate a certain level of ownership, and some
people who buy church bonds may feel as though they
"own" the church. All too often, people with a large investment in ministry bonds are tempted to control that ministry. After all, their interest earnings are at stake.

Remember that interest-bearing bonds are *not gifts*—
they are *investments,* similar in intent and purpose to
stocks, mutual funds, and other investments.[6]

There are other potential dangers: If a ministry has un-
settling problems after bonds are sold, people may demand
their money back before the bonds mature, forcing financial hardship on the ministry. And if the ministry experiences financial problems while the bonds are maturing,

there may not be enough money to pay them off at maturity. Churches can be forced into bankruptcy this way.

A Church Bankrupt. Bankruptcy is exactly what happened some years ago to a large, independent church in upstate South Carolina. With a bus ministry, a Christian school, and a growing congregation, the church had become one of the larger independent churches in its community. Unfortunately, the pastor felt the church had to "compete" against several other large churches in the area.

His competitive attitude drove the pastor to make a series of unwise decisions, culminating in a push to construct a church/school gymnasium. With the church already financially strapped by the burden of paying off earlier loans for the current facility, the pastor decided to sell bonds—at interest—to finance the construction of the new gym.

To persuade the people to approve the bond issue, the pastor frequently preached that the church was in the "last days" before Christ's return. His oft-repeated view was that it didn't matter how much borrowing the church did, as long as the congregation could make its loan payments. He passionately taught that the Rapture of the church would take place very soon, before the loans could ever be paid off. And when the buildings were vacated by the congregation being taken up with Christ, the lenders could do whatever they wanted with the empty facility.

The congregation approved the bond issue. Bonds began to sell, and the gymnasium was built.

However, the pastor's cavalier attitude about money proved to be his undoing—and that of the church, as well. He spent church money frequently, and in large quantities, on any "pet" project that caught his eye. The church's governmental structure was set up in such a way that the pastor was accountable to no one, and his spending continued unabated.

A Bond Panic. Some time after the gymnasium was completed, word began to spread that the church was on shaky financial ground. When several people tried to cash in their bonds early (which was their option, at a loss of interest earnings), they were told that there was no money available. This created a panic, with everyone trying to immediately cash in their bonds.

The church was forced into bankruptcy, the congregation abandoned the pastor, and the church ceased to exist.

For a very long time the church property remained empty, the buildings vacant and deteriorating. After sitting for many years as a blight on both the landscape and the name of Christ, the property was eventually sold and the facility was transformed into a collection of retail businesses.

Admittedly, this church had serious problems, of which the bonds were only a part. However, due to the failure of the bond issue, the church died with a poor testimony, never being able to work out its real problems.

INTEREST-FREE BONDS: A BIBLICAL ALTERNATIVE

Despite the horror stories, we're *not* saying that bonds can *never* be used to fund ministry expansion. Yet these stories and many others like them are all too real and all too common—so be *aware* of the many dangers. Count the cost. If you believe your ministry simply *must* borrow, interest-free bonds are a much better option—and a more biblical option—than either interest-bearing church bonds or borrowing from the unsaved.

Larry Burkett has observed and advised hundreds of churches during more than two decades of non-profit financial ministry. He had this to say in response to a radio caller who had questions about investing in his church's bond program:

> There is nothing inherently wrong with a church bond program. There are a great many risks, however. I do believe if God's people lend money to a church, they should not charge interest for it. There's an Old Testament admonition for God's people not to charge each other interest. I've known an awful lot of church bonds that didn't get paid on time, or didn't get paid at all—in which case you [need] to be able to forgive that.
>
> I'd say if you have free money that you don't need for a substantial period of time, say five years or longer, go ahead and loan [your church] the money—as long as they don't pay you interest. The principle is clear. If we lend money to each

other we are to do it without interest, as a witness to the unsaved around us. [In this way we show] that we are more interested in each other than in the [profit] we might gain
through lending money.[7]

SCRIPTURAL LENDING PRINCIPLES

We've already discussed how God has instructed His
people to be lenders (Psalm 112:5). God says those who
lend freely are "righteous" (Psalm 112:6). In light of God's
clear instruction about lending, we present four principles
for biblical lending. These principles can be especially useful when lending either to fellow Christians or to ministries
(for example, when purchasing church bonds):

- Don't charge interest.
- Expect nothing in return.
- Only lend money you can afford to lose.
- Meet all family needs first.

Don't Charge Interest

As we have previously explained, lending money interest-
free demonstrates godly, self-sacrificial love and conforms
to clear biblical principles.

One of the best examples of the evil of charging interest
among God's people is found in Nehemiah 5:1–13. After
the Jewish exile to Babylon, the new returnees to Jerusalem desperately resorted to borrowing from their countrymen, both to pay the king's tax and to buy food. Because of
the interest they were charging each other, some had already been forced to sell their children into slavery.

God angrily rebuked the people through Nehemiah. Nehemiah heatedly confronted them with the words, "We have
bought back our Jewish brothers who were sold to the Gen-
tiles. Now you are selling your brothers, only for them to
be sold back to us!" (Nehemiah 5:8). The rebuke was met
with silence. The chargers of interest had no defense for
their greed and insensitivity. They repented and returned
everything they had taken.

From the time of Moses, God clearly communicated His desire for generosity to rule the financial relationships of His people. Through Moses, God commanded His people (Exodus 22:25–27) not to charge interest of each other. If collateral was required, a man was not permitted to keep anything his brother truly needed, such as a cloak. If the cloak was taken, it had to be returned by sunset. Why? Because the borrower would need it to stay warm during the night. God then adds an important caution to those who violate this principle: "When he cries out to me, I will hear, for I am compassionate" (v. 27). God wants His people to be compassionate to one another, even as He is compassionate to all His children.

When a ministry (or an individual believer) is in need, a Christian's first response should be to give generously and compassionately, expecting nothing in return. However, if that is impossible or highly impractical and a loan is the only alternative, the loan should be interest-free. Profiting from lending to fellow believers is contrary to everything God has ever expected of His people.

One practical note: Certain tax laws may apply to interest-free loans. Because tax laws constantly change, we recommend you consult a skilled tax adviser about the potential legal issues that relate to interest-free loans. For example, if you lend more than $10,000, be sure to find out whether or not you are required to pay taxes on "phantom" interest.

Expect Nothing in Return

In Luke 6:35, Jesus set an even higher standard than God established under the Old Covenant: One should lend to one's *enemies* "without expecting to get anything back. Then your reward will be great, and you will be sons of the Most High, because he is kind to the ungrateful and wicked."

This is one of the biblical evidences of someone who is "righteous"—lending and expecting nothing back. In other words, Christians should be those who *give*.

However, under certain conditions what you want to lend may be a primary source of income. Suppose you're retired and living on Social Security, with no family to help support you. You own a tract of land that you would prefer to donate to your church. Yet the sale of that property is your only other viable source of retirement income. In this case, as much as you'd like to give the property outright, your very livelihood depends on selling it. You may want to consider having the church make interest-free payments to you, with little or nothing down, for less than seven years. This way the church gets the property with little or no money down and makes payments for only a short time. And in addition to your retirement income, you get the satisfaction of seeing the property used for the work of the ministry.

This is lending that fully conforms to biblical principles.

Only Lend Money You Can Afford to Lose

To be a smart money manager, you need to know how much you can afford to spend—or lose. This is one reason that a personal or family budget is an essential part of wise Christian living. If you don't know how much money you need to live, you'll never be able to calculate how much you can afford to lose. The Bible says, "It is required that those who have been given a trust [e.g., 'managers' or 'stewards'] must prove faithful" (1 Corinthians 4:2).

God has entrusted all of us with resources, and we *must* use them wisely. Many of us have accumulated resources that we have wisely prepared in advance: children's college funds, contingency savings accounts, funds for replacing an aging car, and so forth. Before investing, consider carefully whether it would be wiser to divert these funds to the church or to use them for the original purpose for which you have prepared them.

Please don't misunderstand us: Christians *must* be sacrificial givers. But biblical giving does not mean giving away *everything, all the time.* Even while instructing the Corinthians to give generously, Paul said, *"Our desire is not that others might be relieved while you are hard pressed,* but that there might be equality" (2 Corinthians 8:13, italics added).

In true biblical giving, *everyone* gives generously. That way everyone's needs are met and no one shoulders a disproportionate share of the load.

Meet All Family Needs First

First Timothy 5:8 clearly states: "If anyone does not provide for his relatives, and especially for his immediate family, he has denied the faith and is worse than an unbeliever." The primary function of work is *provision* for one's own family. Be certain you don't jeopardize your family's financial stability by investing in a church bond program (this principle applies to all other investment plans as well).

Build a family budget that both husband and wife agree on—and live by it. As God enables you, provide as best you can for both long- and short-term needs. Then, if you have unallocated discretionary income remaining, invest wisely.

For specific investment principles and guidelines, refer to Larry Burkett's *Investing for the Future* or *Preparing for Retirement;* or Austin Pryor's *Sound Mind Investing.*

THE POWER OF INTEREST-FREE LENDING

Lend correctly and wisely, in accordance with Scripture. Remember that lending is not just a money matter. Woven into the fabric of every loan are people's hopes and dreams. Because money speaks so compellingly, people listen when it talks.

Money can even be a tool to win people to Christ—but not if Christians use it in unbiblical ways. Although it's not an everyday occurrence, God sometimes uses biblical lending to lead people to Himself. In this excerpt from one of Larry Burkett's monthly newsletters, Burkett tells of the powerful impact that interest-free lending can have on the eternal souls of men:

> A Christian businessman . . . shared how God used a non-interest loan to reach an unbeliever. A business acquaintance had experienced a very bad cycle as a result of a recession, and had borrowed against his home to keep his company going. [The unbeliever's] business was growing again, but he was unable to keep his loan current because of the very high inter-

est rate the loan company charged. Knowing he was about to lose his home, the Christian offered to lend him the money [that he needed to keep his loan current] at about half . . . his current rate.

By the time the loan came due, his business was very profitable again, and he was able to pay it off without difficulty. [However], the Christian businessman decided [not to] charge any interest for the loan and had to argue the non-Christian out of paying it. [The Christian businessman's] final argument was the clincher. He told [the non-Christian] that God would bless him far beyond any interest he could make and he didn't want to miss God's blessing.

Within a week, the [non-Christian] businessman was . . . asking questions about Christ and what the Bible had to say about money. Shortly after that, he accepted Christ as his Savior. [And he] made a commitment to increase his giving until it [was] at least 100 times the interest that was forgiven."[8]

NOTES

1. Randy Alcorn, *Money, Possessions, and Eternity* (Wheaton, Ill.: Tyndale, 1989), 311–12.

2. Larry Burkett, *Should Churches Borrow?* (Gainesville, Ga.: Christian Financial Concepts, 1988), 4.

3. Ron Blue, appearing on the "Focus on the Family" radio program, 19 March 1988.

4. J. A. Thompson, *Deuteronomy: An Introduction and Commentary,* in *Tyndale Old Testament Commentaries,* gen. ed. D. J. Wiseman (London, England: InterVarsity Press, 1974), 242.

5. David Pollock, appearing on the "Money Matters" radio program, 31 July 91.

6. Ron Blue, "Should Churches Go Into Debt?" *Master Your Money* (newsletter), August 1989.

7. Larry Burkett, "Money Matters" radio program, 12 August 1991.

8. Larry Burkett, *Your Money in Changing Times* (newsletter), September 1984.

CHAPTER 9

THE DEBT-FREE CHURCH MEMBER
Discovering the Joy of the Debt-Free Family

So far, this book has focused on the body of Christ in its corporate form. But there is a final aspect of non-borrowing ministry that we must address: the finances of the individual church member. That's because at its most basic level, the church is made up not of groups, but of families and individuals (1 Corinthians 12:12).

We believe that the church of Jesus Christ will not be truly financially free until the individual members of the church are financially free. This is a bold assertion—even one that some may find offensive. But we mean no offense. Like non-borrowing ministry, the non-borrowing lifestyle is most often one of joyous faith.

Many Christians actually believe that it is impossible to live in America without borrowing money. But as thousands of families nationwide are proving, that belief is false. God Himself has promised to supply every need for committed, generous people who are sold out to Him (2 Corinthians 8:2–8; Philippians 4:19). The question is: To what extent do we trust Him?

Biblical Financial Principles
of "Borrow-Free" Living

The non-borrowing, financially free life is possible only through living by biblical financial principles. We have found that it is virtually impossible to make a financial misstep when using these ten scriptural principles for handling personal and family finances. They are the principles we ourselves live by, and we've tried to list them here in descending order of priority.

This chapter is but a brief treatment of this vital topic, and by no means do we have all the answers. Many authors discuss these principles in a variety of helpful books; we advise you to consult those books for details. We especially recommend *Money, Possessions, and Eternity* (Randy Alcorn), *Debt-Free Living* (Larry Burkett), and *Master Your Money* (Ron Blue).

Principle 1: Give Everything Back to God

God owns it all. From houses and cars to lawnmowers and shoelaces to children and careers, everything belongs to God. He entrusts material things to· His people for a short time so they have the opportunity to learn maturity, self-control, obedience, and contentment from the experience of being faithful managers (stewards) of His property. Living in the world's most materialistic society often clouds our spiritual perception. We gradually become deceived into thinking of things as "mine" and "ours."

To avoid developing a sense of personal ownership, we recommend a daily surrender of everything God has entrusted to you. Every day, as your feet hit the floor, give everything back to Him. Wife. Husband. Children. Houses. Cars. Hobbies. Careers. Bank accounts. Heirlooms. Surrender all to Him, every day, and then rejoice in what He leaves with you to manage.

Principle 2: Give Faithfully and Cheerfully to God's Work

In 2 Corinthians 9:6–8 Paul says, "Remember this: Whoever sows sparingly will also reap sparingly, and whoever sows generously will also reap generously. Each man should give what he has decided in his heart to give, not reluctantly or under compulsion, for God loves a cheerful giver. And God is able to make all grace abound to you, so that in all things at all times, having all that you need, you will abound in every good work."

Paul urges Christians to adopt a lifestyle of joyous, worshipful, generous giving. But is that what we see in modern American Christianity? Hardly. One significant study indicates that the average Christian family gives only 2.5 percent of its income to Christian work.[1] Another study indicates the amount is 2.9 percent or less.[2]

True biblical giving takes three distinct forms, all of which ought to be an integral, functioning part of a healthy Christian life: tithes, generous gifts, and sacrificial gifts.

Tithes. If the practice of tithing were a college course, it could accurately be called "Giving 101." Although there is no specific New-Testament tithing command, the pattern of giving a tenth is basic and universal, transcending Old and New Testaments, law and grace, Israel and the church, modern day and ancient times. Yet research shows that only a few American Christians give 10 percent or more to their local churches. In fact, only about one-third of Christians even claim to give 10 percent or more.[3] But the importance of proportional giving is clearly taught throughout Scripture.

We believe that tithing is where committed Christians ought to *start* giving. Every Christian is called to surrender everything to God, and the outward evidence of that inner surrender is revealed most fundamentally through tithing.

We believe that to conform to God's principle of proportional giving, the tithe (10 percent) is the place to start. But don't stop there. Continue giving in increasing proportion as God leads. When you give in proportion to your income (10, 20, 30 percent and so forth), God gets more as you make more. Regarding the Christian's regular giving, Paul specifically instructs the church, "each one of you should set aside a sum of money *in keeping with his income*" (1 Corinthians 16:2, italics added). When Jesus observed the poor widow casting her two small coins into the temple treasury (Mark 12; Luke 21), He praised her not for the small amount she contributed, but for the awesome proportion!

In our day and time, the local church is the front-line ministry to which we should pledge our primary financial and spiritual allegiance. If you cannot trust your local church with your tithe, find another church. After all, if you can't trust your church with your money, you can't trust it with your spiritual life (Luke 16:11).

According to researcher Sylvia Ronsvalle, "If church members gave 10 percent, churches would have billions more to spend . . . and would not have to make painful decisions about which programs to cut back or eliminate."[4] In addition, if all American church members would tithe, Ronsvalle believes that all church infrastructure and domestic mission needs could be met, and the poor of the entire world could be fed—all by the American church alone![5] For more on this challenging concept, we recommend John and Sylvia Ronsvalle's thought-provoking book *The Poor Have Faces*.

Generous Gifts. Gifts from generosity come from our surplus, over and above our tithes. Tithes should come right off the top, set aside for the local church before we spend anything else. However, generous gifts come from the money we generate beyond tithes and the cost of basic living. They are born in our deep love for our Savior, who taught us love through His joyous, total giving of Himself (2 Corinthians 9:15; Hebrews 12:2). Generous gifts are aggressively encouraged in Scripture (Ephesians 4:28). Paul boldly states that generous gifts are the evidence of our love for Christ (2 Corinthians 8:13–14).

But generous gifts are not meant to place an ongoing hardship on believers. You may not be able to give to every need that comes along, so trust God to provide through others. Paul said, "Our desire is not that others might be relieved while you are hard pressed, but that there might be equality. At the present time your plenty will supply what they need, so that in turn their plenty will supply what you need" (2 Corinthians 8:13–14).

Before you say "no" to meeting a godly need, be certain that God isn't asking you to step out in faith. God may even want you to give up something you highly value—or even need. That is called sacrifice.

Sacrificial Gifts. Within the context of giving, "sacrifice" means to give up something of real value in worship to God. It is a difficult word for Americans to grasp, much less put into practice. Our affluence insulates us not only from the need to sacrifice but from its benefits.

Sacrifice is perhaps the single greatest sign of a deep commitment to Christ. When you're fully committed to Christ, even poverty won't stand in the way of sacrificial giving. Consider the biblical examples of the poverty-stricken widow of Luke and the poor churches of Macedonia (Luke 21:1–4; 2 Corinthians 8:2–5).

The Hebrew widow and the Macedonian churches had this in common: Despite their poverty, they loved and trusted God so well that they knew He would graciously supply their every need. Our selfish culture shields us from such intimacy with God. The result is that our relationship with God is too often shallow and distant, and we cannot bring ourselves to trust God to provide for our needs. As author John C. Haughey says, "In most of us faith is weak, even defective."[6]

Yet as Christians, we must be prepared to sacrifice anything for God. Remember that Christ loved us enough to sacrifice everything for us.

Principle 3: Develop and Live by an Annual Financial Plan

In other words, live on a budget. Many Christians have preconceptions about budgeting, and most of them are negative. That's unfortunate, because a godly, well-managed, balanced budget can bring more financial peace, security, and godly wealth than most people can imagine. How effective a time manager would you be without a calendar? Similarly, a healthy budget enables you to maximize your money for God's glory.

Budgeting is expense control. The "budget" that both of us live by and recommend is actually an "annual expense control plan." Some say, "We don't make enough money to

have a budget." Our response is, "If your income is that
low, you can't afford not to live on a budget!" That's because the less you make, the more carefully you need to
manage it to make ends meet.

You won't find a detailed budget plan in this book. Many
good books have already been written about effective, godly budgeting. To help you build the simplest, most flexible,
and most useful budget possible, we recommend Larry
Burkett's excellent *Financial Planning Workbook*.

When you develop your plan, do so with prayer. Then
present it to God in prayer. Don't be legalistic about your
financial plan; allow God to work and trust Him for the ultimate outcome. And be prepared to adjust your budget as
God brings financial change into your life.

As you live by a well-made expense-control plan, you'll
begin to discover its many advantages, which include
peace of mind, a more effective prayer life, and a greater
ability to give.

Principle 4: Avoid Borrowing,
Stay Out of Debt, and Use Credit Wisely

Our materialistic culture is like a land of alcoholics. If
you lived in an alcoholic culture and you cared about your
fellow citizens' welfare, you would do your utmost to keep
them away from aicohol. Similarly, America is drunk on
materialism, and easy credit is the bartender who serves us
our drinks with a smile. To make matters worse, most
Christians don't exercise financial temperance. They are
just as drunk with borrowing and debt as their worldly
neighbors.

And American's debt problems are getting more serious:
The Federal Reserve has reported that consumer debt from
all sources has reached a record $980 billion and will soon
top $1 trillion.[7] Because of the debt crunch, fewer families
are able to make their loan payments on time.[8]

Despite the Bible's many cautions against borrowing,
even some Christian financial teachers refuse to take a
strong stand against borrowing ("debt"). Instead, they talk
about "good debt" and "bad debt." Good debt is said to be
when you borrow to purchase things that appreciate (in-

crease) in value, such as a house, an education, or investments (including real estate or rental properties). Bad debt
is when you borrow to purchase consumable goods that
have less or no value after they are used, such as food,
clothes, and vacations.[9]

Avoid Borrowing. We have a different perspective altogether. We firmly believe the committed Christian family
that lives by biblical principles has virtually no need for
loans or borrowing. Regardless of what the business-school
gurus say, borrowing money is not an inescapable part of
life. The best way to avoid borrowing is through faith in
God that is accompanied by wise financial planning and
contentment.

We do agree that there can be certain financial advantages to purchasing your primary residence with credit.
However, we recommend that even house loans always be
as small and as short-term as possible. Also, don't forget
that the most attractive of those advantages (the partial interest deduction) may disappear at any time with changing
tax laws. Remember that all borrowing can go wrong in a
big way, at virtually any time.

Throughout the Bible, borrowing is always discussed in
cautionary terms. Yet despite the many dangers of misus-
ing credit, most Americans implicitly believe that borrowing is "a fact of life."[10] Convinced of that inevitability, many
Christians are doing little or nothing to change.

Stay Out of Debt. By our definition of "debt," you are in
debt when you cannot pay what you have promised to pay.
The Bible clearly states that "The wicked borrow and do
not repay" (Psalm 37:21) and "Let no debt remain outstanding" (Romans 13:8).

The scriptural principle is clear, needing little interpre-
tation: Pay what you owe, and pay on time. With few ex-
ceptions, the only way you can get into debt is through
borrowing.

Use Credit Wisely. All credit is risky. So if you simply
must borrow, secure your loan with collateral. Example:
Purchase an affordable house in an appreciating neighbor-
hood and buy it with a substantial down payment.

Another way to reduce the risk inherent in all borrowing is to set aside liquid funds so you can pay a loan or credit-card bill in full at the due date. Example: Buy computer software through mail-order with money you've previously saved in an appropriate budget category. Remember that credit cards are not the problem; charging items with money you don't have is.

Principle 5: Save Money

Saving money is a vital part of wise biblical stewardship, and in many ways it is the key to non-borrowing living. Savings enables us to live after our productive working years are done. Cash reserves allow us to take care of emergency needs. Consumer savings accounts help build a secure foundation for America's financial institutions. Savings helps our national economy to prosper in the long term. And the accumulated resources of Christians, after they have met their basic needs, is what God uses to fund His ministry around the world (Acts 10:2; Ephesians 4:28).

Proverbs 21:20 contrasts the wise and the foolish: "In the house of the wise are stores of choice food and oil, but a foolish man devours all he has." Note that the wise man saves for future needs. But the fool consumes everything, leaving no reserves to draw upon when needs arise.

Save with a purpose. The practice of purposeful saving is vital to the effective outworking of the Christian life. Only as we generate surplus resources beyond our basic living needs can we help meet others' needs. If we consume all that we have, how can we provide for our families, our relatives, or our neighbors? How can we reach out to our Christian brothers (1 John 3:16–18) if we do not set aside resources beyond our needs? How can we help feed the poor and needy (Matthew 25:31–46) if we set aside nothing to offer them?

Purposeful, godly saving looks ahead, wisely sees a financial need looming on the horizon, and prepares for it. Like the ants extolled in Proverbs 6:6–8, godly saving sets aside the appropriate resources in advance, so upcoming needs can be fully met at the appropriate time.

But as you save for the future, don't hoard. Hoarding is selfish, purposeless accumulation—saving not for a specific goal, but because it makes you "feel" more secure. James doesn't condemn those who prepare wisely for the future. He condemns those who proudly and self-indulgently factor God out of the future (James 5:1–5).

Even godly savings can become hoarding if you're unwilling to give up what you've saved. God may sometimes call you to sacrifice accumulated resources. When you stubbornly refuse to give up your savings to God, or when you fearfully refuse to spend the money you've saved when the need actually arises, you've become a hoarder.

Worry is another sign that you've begun hoarding. Christians are clearly commanded in Scripture not to worry. Matthew 6:25; Philippians 4:6–7; and Luke 21:34 plainly state: "Do not worry." That's because God is the owner; you're simply His steward. God has *everything* well in hand, including your savings—and all your future needs.

Principle 6: Guard Against Envy, Greed, and Materialism

The Bible is replete with financial advice, much of it in the form of warnings. For this brief overview of personal and family financial principles, we've identified what we consider to be the "top three" sins that can destroy a Christian's financial life. We've seen family after family and church after church fractured and even wiped out by these agents of spiritual destruction.

Like most sins, these three do not conquer by blitzkrieg. Rather, they sneak up on you, worming their way first into your thinking, then into your lifestyle. We must all guard daily against them. Otherwise the Enemy will use them to neutralize our effectiveness for Christ.

Envy. Envy is the "resentful awareness of an advantage enjoyed by another, joined with a desire to possess the same advantage." When contentment vanishes, envy tries to fill the vacuum.

Envy denies God's sovereignty. Envy whispers, "God didn't do right by you. See that other guy? Why should he get all the good stuff? God obviously didn't come through for you, so you've got to provide for yourself."

Envy is destructive. Consider these examples of what God says about envy and its results:

- Resentment kills a fool, and envy slays the simple. (Job 5:2)
- A heart at peace gives life to the body, but envy rots the bones. (Proverbs 14:30)
- For [with] envy and selfish ambition, [is] disorder and every evil practice. (James 3:16)

Don't envy what others have. God knows your needs and has your best interests at heart. As the perfect Father, His provision is perfect. He deploys His people into His battlefields as He sees fit, according to the gifts and strengths that He has given to each one. Our advice: Bloom radiantly and contentedly where God has planted you. Give no thought to what others may have.

Greed. In our "modern" society, we don't think of ourselves as idol worshipers. We read in the Bible about how people bowed down to idols, and we think, "Man, were they ignorant!"

In many ways our materialistic culture is no different from the mountain peoples of Papua New Guinea who worship yams. They worship vegetables; we worship dollars. Yet Colossians 3:5 says, "Put to death, therefore, whatever belongs to your earthly nature: sexual immorality, impurity, lust, evil desires and *greed, which is idolatry*" (italics added).

Greed is "excessive or reprehensible acquisitiveness"; in other words, powerfully and selfishly wanting to acquire more and more material things. Greed, like envy, denies the adequacy of God's provision. Greed shouts, "You don't have enough! You'll only be happy with more!"

In our culture, greed isn't generally frowned upon. Rather, our consumer mentality equates "excessive acquisitiveness" with success. Yet God takes a hard line against greed:

- A greedy man stirs up dissension, but he who trusts in the Lord will prosper. (Proverbs 28:25)

- For from within, out of men's hearts, come evil thoughts, sexual immorality, theft, murder, adultery, greed, malice, deceit, lewdness, envy, slander, arrogance and folly. All these evils come from inside and make a man "unclean." (Mark 7:21–23)
- For of this you can be sure: No immoral, impure or greedy person—such a man is an idolater—has any inheritance in the kingdom of . . . God. (Ephesians 5:5)

Someday Christians will stand before the Savior and give an account. Will He chastise us for our greed? Or will He say, "Well done, good and faithful servant"?

Materialism. America is the world's most materialistic society. But as Randy Alcorn correctly points out, materialism is not just a "yuppie" disease—it's an ailment of the human soul, to which anyone living in a fallen world is susceptible:

> Materialism begins with what we believe. Not merely what we say we believe, not our doctrinal statement, but the philosophy of life we actually live by. Hence, [even the Christian may] be preoccupied with material rather than spiritual things and therefore in fact be a practicing materialist.
>
> A materialist may be rich or poor, own much or little, be a miser or a spendthrift. Materialism . . . is first and foremost a matter of the heart.[11]

Materialism may well be the toughest financial (and spiritual) issue for the American church to deal with. That's because we're so steeped in our intensely materialistic culture that materialism is all we know. For most Americans, including most Christians, materialism is the norm.

But we must not give in. Only as we free ourselves from the self-imposed shackles of "thing-worship" can we redirect our vast resources toward meeting the needs of people (who, unlike things, will last forever). The battle against materialism must be waged daily, minute by minute, thought by thought. And it can only be won through a daily recommitment and resurrender to God.

Principle 7: Learn to Be Content

Luke chapter 3 tells how John the Baptist preached in the wilderness as Christ's forerunner. People from all walks of life responded to his challenge to "produce fruit in keeping with repentance" (v. 8). It's significant that when the crowd asked, "What should we do?" (v. 10), John gave financial advice. He commanded generous sharing (v. 11) and financial integrity (v. 13): "Then some soldiers asked him, 'And what should we do?' He replied, 'Don't extort money and don't accuse people falsely—be content with your pay.'" (v. 14). Just imagine the "godly" works John could have encouraged those Roman soldiers to perform. Instead, his counsel focused on their attitudes: Don't be greedy; don't be untruthful; be content.

The writer of Proverbs said, "The fear of the Lord leads to life: Then one rests content, untouched by trouble" (19:23). In modern America, Christians know little of contentment. The constant materialistic blare of our culture drowns out the still, small voice of contentment.

We have learned through serving as financial counselors that a lack of contentment is one of the primary reasons for financial problems. Lack of contentment is perhaps the primary cause for most borrowing and debt, in families as well as ministries. The writer of Proverbs knew that reverence for God was at the core of a contented life. A thousand years later, the apostle Paul expressed the same view in slightly different words: "Godliness with contentment is great gain" (1 Timothy 6:6).

What's the secret of contentment? Paul discovered it, and he shared it with his Philippian friends. Expressing his joy over their financial support, he said, "I have learned to be content whatever the circumstances. I know what it is to be in need, and . . . to have plenty. I have learned the secret of being content in . . . every situation, whether well fed or hungry, whether living in plenty or in want. I can do everything through him who gives me strength" (Philippians 4:11–13).

Paul was saying, "I've gone hungry, and I've eaten my fill. Sometimes I've done without; on other occasions I've had much more than I've needed. Through these cycles of emptying and filling, God has taught me to trust Him; to be content. Whatever my financial condition, I can handle it for God's glory, because He gives me the strength I need, when I need it." Contentment is an inner confidence, based on knowing the perfect character of God and trusting in His wise provision. It has been said that "contentment is realizing that God has already provided everything we need for our present happiness." We agree.

Principle 8: Have the Right Motives

No discussion of principles could be complete without examining motives. From an eternal perspective (the proper perspective of all Christians), there are two healthy motives for wanting to live by biblical financial principles: love and accountability.

Love. As a result of His gift of eternal salvation, our love for God should so overwhelm us that our highest desire is to please Him. Those who love God should be motivated to obey and follow Him (John 14:15, 21). Throughout His Word, God commands that we handle our material resources wisely. Through Christ, God made the ultimate sacrifice for us (John 3:16; 2 Corinthians 8:9). Our love for Him motivates us to manage His resources wisely.

True love for God is not feeling, but action. And the action that defines love for God is giving. First John 3:16–19 says that loving as Christ does means sacrificing your own life for others by giving your resources to those in need. Then you'll confidently know you "belong to the truth."

Accountability. Accountability is the other healthy motive for living by biblical financial principles. This is especially important when we consider eternity. Someday believers will stand before God (1 Corinthians 3:11–15). When our works as believers are tested by God Himself, will they endure? Will we hear Him say, "Well done, good and faithful servant! Come and share your master's happiness" (Matthew 25:21, 23)? Or will our works, done in our own strength to satisfy ourselves, be destroyed by fire? Knowing the awesome impact of our eternal accountability should motivate us to serve Him with a singular commitment to excellence. John Wesley said, "I value all things only by the price they shall gain in eternity."[12]

Principle 9: Plan Wisely

Chapter 6 explains that godly planning is good, wise, scriptural, and necessary for successful ministry. We won't repeat what was said there about the importance of planning, but we must stress the importance of wise, balanced planning from a personal and family perspective.

Note that you don't truly have a plan unless it's measurable and it's achievable. So put your plans in writing, and set goals that you can actually measure—and achieve. As with ministry planning, we're not suggesting that you make rigid, inflexible plans that cannot be changed. If you do that, you'll leave no room for God to work in your life.

Short-Range Plans. Godly planning begins with a personal or family budget. As we have already said, a budget is a relatively short-range plan, extending in time only a year or so. Because circumstances change, it's especially important not to become legalistic about short-term plans. Think of your budget as a maturing child: living, changing, and growing with you as your stewardship skills build in strength over time. So write your budget plans in pencil. Then, as God leads and guides, use the eraser.

Medium-Range Plans. You should also build medium-range plans—those extending from one to five years. Things such as house remodeling, family reunion trips, automobile replacement, and optional major appliance purchases are some of the normal financial burdens that you should prepare and begin saving for several years in advance. And as you identify your medium-range plans, be sure to incorporate them into your short-range goals.

Long-Range Plans. Long-range goals (those beyond five years) can include such things as private education, higher education, weddings, graduations, retirements, and funerals. And if you haven't taken the time to calculate the cost of long-range goals, you'll have no idea how to financially prepare to reach them. That's why, more so than with any other kind of plan, your long-range plans must be highly flexible. You'll also need to periodically adjust your plans for changing economic conditions, such as inflation or recession.

Whether it's discipleship or retirement, the principle remains true: Count the cost, lest you fail and be ashamed (Luke 14:26–33). Plan wisely and prayerfully, let God work, and act in obedient response as He leads. God honors flexible, wise plans that are fully committed to His glory.

Principle 10: Ask for Help

The final of the ten principles is: Don't be afraid to ask for help. After all, Scripture says that "plans fail for lack of counsel, but with many advisers, they succeed" (Proverbs 15:22).

When we (the authors) were growing up in the fifties and sixties, there was no training or help available in the area of biblical financial principles. There wasn't much need for it. Financial management counselor Gene Frost, Jr. explains why:

> Other than a mortgage and a car loan, couples in our parents' generation didn't use much credit. If they needed a washing machine or a new sofa, they waited until they could save enough money to pay cash. They avoided consumer debt, and debt is the greatest burden today's couples struggle with.
>
> If you watch reruns of *The Honeymooners* you'll see what a '50s couple needed—a small apartment with a sink, a stove, a refrigerator, a table with three or four chairs, and a few other pieces of furniture. But if you watch the sitcoms today you see families living in luxurious $300,000 or $400,000 homes. And that is presented as what today's family "needs."[13]

In today's financially stressed, debt-burdened American church, the need for solid biblical financial training is more critical than at perhaps any other time in our nation's history. Fortunately, God has raised up (and continues to raise up) godly financial teachers, counselors, and ministries to serve His people in their time of crisis. For a helpful list of personal and family financial resources (including addresses and phone numbers), refer to the appendix.

This brief treatment of these ten biblical financial principles only scratches the surface of this deep and important subject. If we've piqued your interest, be sure to refer to the books we recommended. Our point is that if you live by these principles, you'll enjoy financial freedom. You'll very seldom (if ever) need to borrow, and you'll be much better prepared to serve the Lord in any capacity He calls you to.

MATERIALISM HINDERS OUTREACH

In our description of financial principle six, we urged Christians to avoid materialism and we presented a biblical case against it. But there's another compelling reason to fight materialism: It hinders our Christian outreach.

Unfortunately, materialism is on the rise among America's Christians. Research repeatedly demonstrates that the material beliefs and values of the average professing Christian are no less selfish and materialistic than those of his ungodly neighbors and co-workers. Christian and non-Christian studies confirm and reconfirm that more people than ever before in our nation's history believe that the church is losing its influence in our society.[14]

This has not always been the case. In his recent book *The Tragedy of American Compassion,* Dr. Marvin Olasky explains how once—until the 1930s—the American church was highly valued as the compassionate "glue" that held our nation's communities together in times of need. He says that "we had a very effective war on poverty in the United States before the federal government got involved. The war was actually led by the church, by Christians."[15]

Yet modern Christians lack a commitment to serve and worship Christ with their resources and finances. In their rush to accumulate things, God's people waste God's resources on luxuries and indulgences. As a result, little is left over to meet the needs in our own churches, much less the lost in our communities—or in foreign lands.

Our preoccupation with luxuries is seriously hindering our ability to have an outreach impact on the lost world. In addition, many Christians are so enslaved to lenders that they find it almost impossible to support even the home-base ministries of their own local churches. Through Christ, we have the power to change (Philippians 4:12–13). But do we have the commitment?

HARD TIMES MAY BE COMING

There's a final reason why financial freedom is so important: Many economic experts agree that America is on the verge of hard economic times. Some speak of a depression so severe as to make the so-called "Great Depression" of the 1930s seem insignificant. Others predict severe recession as industries downsize, consolidate, and relocate to countries with less restrictive economic policies. Still others predict total economic collapse. Even liberal estimates foresee the total depletion of Social Security funding before 2029, which will be during the peak years of "baby boomer" retirement.[16]

Experts such as Larry Burkett, Harry Figgie, and others may disagree about the details, extent, and timing of our potential economic woes, but they do agree in one key area: If America does nothing to reverse its runaway debt and spending trends, our nation may very likely experience deep economic hardship, possibly within the lifetime of today's baby boomers.

Some dismiss dire economic predictions as the product of conservative Christian alarmists. It is certainly a betrayal of the Christian faith to become fearful, discouraged, or depressed over what might happen in the future (Hebrews 13:5–6). On the other hand, it's just as unwise to throw financial caution to the winds. Even the International Monetary Fund (a decidedly non-Christian organization) predicts difficult economic times for America if our nation does not get its debt problem under control.[17]

This book champions the cause of non-borrowing ministry. However, we too often think of ministry as something done by church groups or parachurch organizations. As a result, we gradually forget that ministry means *serving*. And the greatest ministry known is that of a godly family or individual reaching out to help hurting people. But when hard times come, loan-encumbered Christians will struggle to cope. Many non-borrowing Christians, however, will be able to have a powerful witness.

Whether or not an economic cataclysm occurs in America, hard economic times still seem to visit us every decade or so. And history has proven repeatedly that Christ's church performs at its peak not when it is fat and happy, but when it is tested in the heat of hardship and persecution. When America's next economic hardship rolls into your community, will you be financially positioned to minister—or to be ministered to?

TAKE ACTION

Don't be lax in either your church or personal finances. Study God's Word carefully. Develop your own financial convictions. If you need help, counsel, or training, get it. Don't let pride or a hectic schedule interfere with becoming a wise steward. Live by biblical principles, and trust God to meet your needs as you remain diligent, generous, and content.

Whatever you do, don't assume that a simple lack of funds is an automatic reason to borrow at interest. Ask for godly wisdom, pray about the matter, look for alternatives, and be prepared to accept God's answer, even if His answer is "no," "wait," or simply "do without."

The journey toward the debt-free church begins and ends with debt-free families. It's a fascinating trip, sometimes frustrating, sometimes challenging, but always rewarding and spiritually invigorating. It's a journey you'll never regret. Why not begin today?

NOTES

1. "Members Get Richer But Not the Churches," *Orlando Sentinel,* 31 December 1994, D–5.

2. David Briggs, "Study Shows Roman Catholics Give Less Than 1 Percent of Income to Fund Church," *Houston Post,* 26 December 1992.

3. George Barna and William Paul McKay, *Vital Signs* (Westchester, Ill.: Crossway, 1984), 112.

4. "Members Get Richer But Not the Churches," *Orlando Sentinel,* 31 December 1994, D-5.

5. John Ronsvalle and Sylvia Ronsvalle, *The Poor Have Faces* (Grand Rapids: Baker, 1992), 45.

6. John C. Haughey, *The Holy Use of Money* (Garden City, N.Y.: Doubleday, 1986), 2.

7. Jerry Jackson, "Consumer Debt Climbing Faster Than Income Rate," *Orlando Sentinel,* 21 September 1995, B-1.

8. Ibid.

9. Daniel D. Busby, Kent E. Barber, and Robert L. Temple, *The Christian's Guide to Worry-Free Money Management* (Grand Rapids: Zondervan, 1994), 70.

10. Judith Briles, *Judith Briles' Money Guide for Christian Women* (Ventura, Calif.: Regal Books, 1991), 86.

11. Randy Alcorn, *Money, Possessions, and Eternity* (Wheaton, Ill.: Tyndale, 1989), 54.

12. Ibid., 125.

13. "Making Ends Meet," *Marriage Partnership,* Summer 1995 (accessed via America Online).

14. Ronsvalle, *The Poor Have Faces,* 58.

15. "Getting a God's Eye View of Reality," *Reformed Quarterly,* Summer 1995, 10.

16. David Stahl, "The Savings Problem," *America's Community Banker,* April 1995, 17.

17. Stephen A. Davies, "IMF Sees Debt Holding Back U.S. Economy," *American Banker,* 4 May 1995, 26.

"While renting has its advantages, it is the opinion of the deacons that we start a building fund."

AFTERWORD

In this book we have tried to challenge the church that God's best plan and highest direction for ministry is to avoid borrowing and remain debt-free. It's our hope and prayer that all Christian ministries might someday be set free from the financial bondage that borrowing brings.

Thousands of Christian ministries across America have discovered the joy that comes from trusting God to sovereignly supply every ministry need. Yet other ministries continue to borrow, and in so doing actually hinder themselves from seeing God work near-miraculous feats of glorious provision.

We continually ask ourselves how Christians can legitimately claim to believe that God meets every need for every good work (2 Corinthians 9:8) and then use worldly financing methods to fund ministry. God has given the church an approved method for meeting ministry needs: the generous, sacrificial giving of believers. God has even provided funding examples and models in His Word. And in every biblical example of God-funded ministry, God's people gave before the work started, and in such sufficiency they often had to be told to stop. The concept of borrowing and making payments is simply not found in Scripture. Our conclusion, as narrow as it may seem to some, is that borrowing is almost never God's will for funding the work of ministry.

Furthermore, ministries that borrow too often find themselves in debt, and thereby open themselves up to all manner of problems and temptations. Ministries that are in debt often discover that their financial bondage prevents them from accomplishing much of the work that God has intended them to do. And if the Lord delays His return and the economy worsens, untold suffering may be ahead for ministries that have borrowed. Rather than borrowing, the church must teach believers to trust God, deny materialism, and give sacrificially. With the abundant supply provided by true biblical giving, no ministry will ever lack full funding.

But a debt-free ministry conviction must be founded in more than just the fear of doomsday predictions. When a ministry commits to no borrowing, that ministry enters the wonderful realm of complete financial dependence on God. As God reveals creative ministry methods to them, leaders of debt-free, balanced ministries can begin to explore innovative ministry methods and opportunities that they may never before have considered. Debt-free ministry is not an easy road, and ministering debt-free necessitates aggressive dependence on the heavenly Father.

Borrowing may be the easiest way to fund ministry, but it is not the best way. In fact, borrowing ought to be a last resort. Yet if you do find yourself in a situation in which borrowing is unavoidable, be sure to follow the scriptural borrowing and lending guidelines we presented in chapter 8.

Debt-free ministries will never be the norm until debt-free believers are the norm. To fully honor God's biblical financial principles, it's essential that both individuals and families commit to becoming and remaining debt-free. The church of Jesus Christ will never be truly financially free until the individual members of His church are debt-free. And by God's grace, it's happening.

In the final analysis, godly ministry is not a question of what "works." Rather, the question to ask is, "Are we consistently conforming ourselves to biblical principles?" It's true that there are many stories about ministries that have struggled or have even gone out of existence as a result of the negative consequences of borrowing. Some of those stories are in this book. But for all the negative examples there are other cases in which ministries have borrowed and continued to grow.

What are we to conclude? We must realize that apparent ministry success or failure doesn't validate either the pro-borrowing or the anti-borrowing position. Only God, from His eternal perspective, can determine true success. God commands us to follow Him, whether or not we understand Him, agree with His wisdom, or even perceive any benefit. Our responsibility—our spiritual duty—is to consistently live by biblical principles.

Some say, "There are ministries that borrow and do well. Those ministries are proof that borrowing can be beneficial." That argument is invalid. It's like using those who practice an unhealthy lifestyle and live to old age as proof that dissipation is the secret to longevity.

God's financial principles are intended for our benefit, and there are no cases in Scripture where God commends borrowing. In fact, every biblical reference to borrowing is either a caution, a warning, or a curse. Do Christians really want to fund ministry with methods that God frowns upon?

When Christians disregard God's principles, they put themselves at risk and in danger of suffering the consequences of their actions. We believe that the avoidance of borrowing is one of God's clearest financial principles. We urge our fellow believers to stop borrowing to fund ministry. Instead, trust God to supply all your ministry needs through the generous and sacrificial giving of His people.

In 1835 George Mueller began a ministry to orphans in Bristol, England. Until his death in 1898, millions of dollars passed through his hands. Yet Mueller never made a single public request for financial support, either for himself or his ministry. By faith, Mueller saw God again and again supply all the needs of a ministry that ultimately had worldwide impact. Mueller also had a firm conviction against ministry borrowing, which he once expressed in the colorful manner of his day:

If the work in which we are engaged is indeed the work of God, then . . . He will provide the means for it at the time they are needed. I do not mean that He will provide them when we think that they are needed, but . . . when there is real need. . . . We trust God to supply us with what we require at present, so that there may be no need for going into debt. . . . The living God is ready to prove Himself as the living God . . . so that we need not go away from Him . . . to the ways of the world. . . . He is both able and willing to supply us with all that we can need in His service.[1]

NOTE

1. George Mueller, *Autobiography of George Müller: The Life of Trust,* ed. H. Linclon Wayland (Grand Rapids: Baker, 1981; previously published as *The Life of Trust,* Boston: Gould and Lincoln, 1861), 242–43.

HELPFUL RESOURCES FOR DEBT-FREE LIVING

A wide range of resources exists to help families and ministries in the process of becoming financially free. This appendix provides background information, addresses, and phone numbers for well-balanced Christian resources that can provide materials, publications, seminars, video instruction, and even computer budgeting software. These brief profiles are by no means all-inclusive, nor are these the only resources available.

So if you're struggling financially, don't let pride or ignorance stand in your way. Get the help you need. Free resource information is available from each of these organizations on request.

Christian Financial Concepts. Perhaps the best-known among Biblical-finance teachers and ministries is Larry Burkett and his debt-free, nondenominational, nonprofit ministry, Christian Financial Concepts (CFC). In the course of more than twenty years of ministry, Burkett has written dozens of books. CFC has trained thousands of volunteer budget counselors, who counsel and teach under the direction and authority of their local churches. Many thousands of others have been through CFC video seminars, have completed CFC Bible-study and budgeting workbooks, or use CFC's budgeting software. CFC radio broadcasts are heard on more than a thousand radio stations nationwide. The ministry also offers practical, Bible-based financial seminars for families, businessmen, pastors, and those seeking career guidance.

For more information, contact:

Christian Financial Concepts
601 Broad Street, S.E.
Gainesville, GA 30501-3729
Phone: (770) 534-1000
Toll-Free Order Line: (800) 722-1976

Crown Ministries. Crown Ministries is an interdenominational, nonprofit ministry that employs an effective small-group study to train Christians how to apply biblical financial principles in their daily lives. The studies are conducted through churches and communities across America and in several foreign countries. The twelve-week study covers biblical financial principles and teaches a budgeting system. Some of the Crown distinctives are Scripture memorization, an emphasis on prayer, and accountability. Printed materials are also available.

For more information, contact:

Crown Ministries, Inc.
530 Crown Oak Centre Drive
Longwood, FL 32750
Phone: (407) 331-6000

Eternal Perspective Ministries. Directed by author and former pastor Randy Alcorn, the Eternal Perspective Ministries' purpose is two-fold: to teach biblical principles from an eternal viewpoint and to reach the needy for Christ by helping the local church. One of Alcorn's many superb books is *Money, Possessions, and Eternity,* which may be the finest and most challenging exposition of biblical financial principles currently available. The ministry also offers a free newsletter called *Eternal Perspective,* and Alcorn is available for speaking engagements and seminars.

For more information, contact:

Eternal Perspective Ministries
2229 East Burnside 23
Gresham, OR 97080
Phone: (503) 663-6481

No-Debt Living Newsletter. Editor Bob Frank's monthly
No-Debt Living newsletter is a professional and affordable
resource that is filled with a wealth of information, suggestions, and strategies for Christians who want to do all they
can to experience debt-free living. From wedding advice to
car-buying tips, from coupon-clipping to stock analysis,
No-Debt Living is a superb and unique resource for helping
maintain a non-borrowing lifestyle. Frank is also available
for speaking engagements and seminars. An evaluation
copy of the newsletter is available on request.
For more information, contact:

No-Debt Living Newsletter
Post Office Box 282
Veradale, WA 99037
Phone: (509) 927-1322
Toll-Free: (800) 560-3328

Ronald Blue & Co. Financial and investment expert Ron
Blue has written numerous books on biblical financial principles, including several with his wife Judy. Blue's materials cover such subjects as women's finances, biblical
financial principles for children, national economic per-
spectives, and resolving money conflicts in marriage.
Whereas Ronald Blue & Co. is a for-profit financial-man-
agement and investment-counseling firm that works with
private individuals and institutions on a fee-only basis,
Blue's materials are excellent and well worth your investment in them. Also available is the entertaining and engag-
ing *Master Your Money* video series, which can be
presented in adult Sunday-school classes or home-study
groups.

For more information, contact:

Ronald Blue & Co.
Attention: Marketing
1100 Johnson Ferry Road, Suite 600
Atlanta, GA 30342
Phone: (404) 705-7000

Sound Mind Investing. Austin Pryor's excellent monthly newsletter, *Sound Mind Investing,* is becoming increasingly well-known as a result of his book of the same name and his many guest appearances on Larry Burkett's live, call-in radio program, *Money Matters.* A former investment adviser who gave up his investment business to write and publish his newsletter, Pryor's financial advice is both practical and biblically based. Highly recommended.

For more information, contact:

Sound Mind Investing
Post Office Box 22128-M
Louisville, KY 40252-0128
Phone: (502) 426-7420

BIBLIOGRAPHY

Alcorn, Randy. *Money, Possessions, and Eternity.* Wheaton, Ill.: Tyndale, 1989.

Barna, George. *Virtual America.* Ventura, Calif.: Regal, 1994.

Barna, George and William Paul McKay. *Vital Signs.* Westchester, Ill.: Crossway, 1984.

Blue, Ron. *Master Your Money.* Nashville: Thomas Nelson, 1986.

Bowman, Ray, with Eddy Hall. *When Not to Build.* Grand Rapids: Baker, 1992.

Burkett, Larry. *Debt-Free Living.* Chicago: Moody, 1989.

_____. *Financial Planning Workbook.* Chicago: Moody, 1990.

_____. *How to Manage Your Money.* Chicago: Moody, 1982.

_____. *Investing for the Future.* Wheaton, Ill.: Scripture Press, 1992.

_____. *Preparing for Retirement.* Chicago: Moody, 1992.

_____. *Should Churches Borrow?* (pamphlet). Gainesville, Ga.: Christian Financial Concepts, 1988.

_____. *Using Your Money Wisely: Guidelines from Scripture.* Chicago: Moody, 1985.

_____. *The Word on Finances.* Chicago: Moody, 1994.

_____. *Your Finances in Changing Times.* Chicago: Moody, 1982.

Busby, Daniel D., Kent E. Barber, and Robert L. Temple. *The Christian's Guide to Worry-Free Money Management.* Grand Rapids: Zondervan, 1994.

Eklund, Bob, and Terry Austin. *Partners with God: Bible Truths About Giving.* Nashville: Convention, 1995.

Fooshee, George and Marjean. *Your Money.* Uhrichsville, Ohio: Barbour and Co., 1994.

Getz, Gene. *A Biblical Theology of Material Possessions.* Chicago: Moody, 1990.

Hales, Edward J. and J. Alan Youngren. *Your Money, Their Ministry.* Grand Rapids: Eerdmans, 1981.

Haughey, John C. *The Holy Use of Money.* Garden City, N.Y.: Doubleday, 1986.

Martin, Malachi. *Rich Church, Poor Church.* New York: G. P. Putnam's Sons, 1984.

Pryor, Austin. *Sound Mind Investing.* Chicago: Moody, 1993.

Ronsvalle, John and Sylvia. *The Poor Have Faces.* Grand Rapids: Baker, 1992.

_____. *The State of Church Giving Through 1992.* Champaign, Ill.: empty tomb, inc., 1994.

Moody Press, a ministry of the Moody Bible Institute,
is designed for education, evangelization, and edification.
If we may assist you in knowing more about Christ
and the Christian life, please write us without obligation:
Moody Press, c/o MLM, Chicago, Illinois 60610.